Thames & Hudson

Scripts

Elegant Lettering from Design's Golden Age

Steven Heller and Louise Fili

First published in 2011 in hardcover in the United States of America by
Thames & Hudson Inc., 500 Fifth Avenue, New York, New York 10110

thamesandhudsonusa.com

First paperback edition 2012
Reprinted 2015

Library of Congress Catalog Card Number 2010936806
ISBN 978-0-500-29039-2

Printed and bound in China by C & C Offset Printing Co. Ltd

Contents

....

INTRODUCTION
6

FRENCH · SCRIPTES
12

BRITISH · SCRIPTS
90

GERMAN · DIE SCHRIFT
114

ITALIAN · IL CORSIVO
146

AMERICAN · SCRIPTS
236

FURTHER READING
350

෴

Elegance & Eccentricity

"NO ONE PERSON EVER INVENTED AN ALPHABET," TYPE GURU SAMUEL WINFIELD (TOMMY) THOMPSON WROTE in *The Script Letter: Its Form, Construction and Application* (1955). Script typefaces were no exception. During the letterpress era they were in such great demand that many people "invented" them, and many others copied them. In some commercial printing shops composing cases filled with scripts were stacked floor to ceiling to the exclusion of other typefaces. Printers routinely amassed multiple styles of the heavy-metal fonts, each possessing a distinct twist, flourish, or quirk used to inject a hint of personality or dash of character to everyday printed pieces. The faces had names like Wedding Plate Script, Cursive Script, Engraver's Script, Bank Script, Master Script, French Script, Stationers Semiscript, and Myrtle Script (*myrtle?*). There were countless others. They surfaced in Europe and America—basically anywhere Latin type was used. And the exact same typefaces as were used in France, for example, could be found in Italian foundries, but with different names.

Since they approximated and mimicked handwriting, script typefaces were *de rigueur* for weddings, births, graduations, and anniversaries. Almost any kind of formal or personal announcement and invitation was routinely composed with ornate scripts, including calling cards, business cards, dance cards, letterheads, billheads, prescriptions, bank drafts, diplomas, and certificates. Product labels and packaging were also given the script treatment. Scripts signaled propriety, suggested authority, yet also exuded status and a bourgeois aesthetic. The wealthy classes couldn't get enough fashionable scripts in their diet. Likewise, the nouveau riche embraced them too—maybe they thought it helped them to appear even wealthier.

Scripts were at once decorative and symbolic—the quintessence of class and classiness. Yet their ultimate widespread availability and accessibility to anyone who wanted to use them eventually made scripts classless and déclassé. Nonetheless, they never completely went out of style—and they naturally come back again and again, albeit often as a novelty.

Script type was developed "to its finest stage of beauty," wrote Tommy Thompson in *The Script Letter*, "during the 17th and 18th centuries by European penmen and engravers." The one man he singles out for the highest respect is George Bickham the Elder (1684–1758), who in 1741 published *The Universal Penman*, a veritable pantheon of great penmen's works to that date. Thompson notes that, "Little has been contributed to the design of the script letter since Bickham's time save to cast its forms into type and, I must add, to tighten and often distort the characters to the will of the machine." Indeed, Bickham's *Universal Penman* is to script lettering what Giambattista Bodoni's *Manuale Tipografico* (1818) is to Roman letters.

Speaking of which, if Roman type is "official" lettering and handwriting is "informal" lettering, then script typefaces are perhaps the bastard (but not feral) children of both. The thing about scripts—and every schoolchild before the advent of the computer will attest to this—is that from the early 19th century, strict rules for handwriting, the inspiration for script typefaces, were set down in penmanship primers and handbooks. Many knuckles were rapped with a ruler when these standards were ignored by rebellious kids. So it could be said that script types were born in the crucible of human suffering, and perhaps also in the boudoir of pleasure ...

Writing the perfect script was indeed a chore for the uncoordinated (just try to achieve consistently the 54-degree slope that defines the essential script), and a joy for others, especially forming those sensuous flourishes. Thompson wrote, "No two penmen or lettering men, to my knowledge, have used them in the same manner. They remain a personal element."

Achieving perfection was the holy grail, and one of the most comprehensive guides, published over a century after Bickham's, was *Real Pen Work* (author unknown, 1881), which boasted "more Copies, more Ornamental Work, and more and better Instructions, for learning the Whole Art of Penmanship without a teacher, than any other work ever published in the World." Such bald-faced hyperbole notwithstanding, perfecting script writing was considered a lofty virtue worth the effort. Making words flow off the pen gracefully was on a par with the Platonic ideal.

One "testimonial" published in *Real Pen Work* about a hardworking penman states: "Such Wonderful Improvement must seem more a fairy dream than a reality to anyone who never saw this Self-Instructor ... it is easy enough to learn to write well when you have the proper instruction." Yet the real secret for making elegant scripts lies in the hand, according to the author of *Real Pen Work*:

> Take the pen in the hand between the thumb and the first and second fingers in such a manner that the holder shall cross the first finger just above the knuckle joint. Let the second finger drop below the first so that the holder shall cross it at the root of the nail. The third and fourth fingers should curve beneath the hand and rest upon the nails. This is the most natural method for holding the pen, for when at rest the hand invariably assumes this position ... [After getting the correct position,] it requires but very little practice to be able to do all this kind of work.

From these everyday handwritten letters typefaces were born, and arguably the more typeface styles that were produced the less need there was to write a perfectly elegant letter by hand. Progress works in strange and wonderful ways.

During the golden age of modern script typefaces—roughly from the early 19th through the mid-20th centuries—selecting the perfect script typeface was like choosing the perfect bonnet. Gilt-edged, leather-bound tomes showing how to use scripts properly were abundant. Printers would whet the appetites of script-hungry customers by placing these thick albums, swollen with embossed and debossed specimens of cards and envelopes for all occasions, before their impressionable eyes. Meticulously composed and often printed on ultra-fine papers or heavy-card stock, these "specimen books" were bibles of the commercial genre known as social printing, a service that was then (and to a certain extent still is) the essential media supplier for members and wannabes of polite society. Today these volumes serve as historical records of the manners and mores of their times, as expressed through a range of standardized printed stationery. For the typography connoisseur, though merely well-thumbed, commonplace sales tools, they are as highly valued as any rare book.

Scripts did not, however, satisfy only high society's needs and protocols. They were the typefaces of choice for all kinds of business, large and small. Many logos and trademarks were designed using scripts as the primary or secondary lettering style. Before the advent of modern logo design, scripts gave the illusion that the business name was a signature. They made the impersonal personal. Most trademark scripts were custom made; others were taken from the many templates or "cuts" that were produced by printing firms of the time. Several were of stunning complexity, but just as many were rather mundane, even by standards of the day.

During the 1920s and 1930s, scripts had already gone in and out of fashion a few times. While the Ford Motor Company retained (and continues to jealously guard) its script trademark, many machine-age corporations felt scripts were too quaint for an increasingly sophisticated business world. Instead, scripts found another prodigious medium. In the United States, in particular, but throughout the industrialized commercial world, newspaper and magazine advertisements and posters were loaded with scripts. They were perfect for promoting commodities directly aimed at the leading consuming class and gender—women.

So-called "perfume" scripts provided an accent to headings or running text, the sinuous lines exuding allure and sex appeal. Signaling femininity and social élan, scripts appealed to women subconsciously, and with Pavlovian predictability women found them mouthwatering. These perfume scripts also became endemic to the entire Art Deco phenomenon. They spoke, as much as a typeface can, directly to the female need to be pampered and catered to. Such faces as Raleigh Cursive and Pompeian Cursive, among the many with exotic auras, evoked luxury and exclusivity when they were used on the packaging of soap and shampoo, on hankies or silk stockings. But these frou-frou applications were not the ultimate destination for curvilinear letters. Avant-garde artists and designers had other ideas.

Scripts emerged as planned anachronisms in Dada and Futurist art and design. Experimental modern typographers used bank and society scripts as critical commentary on both the state of art and societal regulations. The Neue Typographie codifier, Jan Tschichold, also had a formal rationale: he used scripts to contrast with his bold sans serifs. What could be more purposefully counter-intuitive? It was a direct slap in the face of typographic propriety and convention.

In the 1930s through the 1950s, a sizeable number of brand-new and revived scripts were introduced for everyday uses or what was known as "commercial handwriting." Some were quite elegant, though many were derived from rough handwriting or heavy brushstrokes. Tommy Thompson noted in *The Script Letter* that "in order to draw a particular style of letter, you must know and choose the tool that most closely approximates the weight of the letter you wish to execute." Don't make a tool do something it was not meant to do, he warned. Today, however, misuse and accident are part of the experimental credo.

Some script faces were just used randomly to add typographic variety to a page; others were used in place of the bold gothic workhorses. In commercial contexts, a script would never be used for, say, a railway sign or other official posting, but it was common and appropriate for virtually any other type of signage, such as grocery or sale signs, which demanded an ad hoc or handwritten appearance. "Technically these styles are neither writing nor lettering," Thompson admonished. But however it is defined, the advent of script lettering and type has been of immeasurable benefit to graphic design for many long years.

The scripts displayed in this book are culled from hundreds of sources, including specimen books, magazines, newspapers, adverts, stationery, and packaging. Taken from the early part of the 20th century, when scripts had the most flair and flourish, they were principally used in five countries: France, Britain, Germany, Italy, and the United States. The word "script" suggests joined-up letters, although in some typefaces the letters don't connect—these are included as faux scripts. Some scripts were workhorses; others were special and sold to the trade with all the accompanying fanfare of a top-ten song or novel. ❧

UNICA
TORINO

Friola

Assortimento
Biscotti finissimi

yz

fai fio

French

IN LA BELLE FRANCE, MOST OF THE BELLE SCRIPT LETTERING AND TYPEFACES—AND THERE ARE MANY iterations—were stylistically influenced by Art Moderne (Art Deco). A preference for ornate cursives among French printers and typographers first developed from those eccentric Art Nouveau vines and tendrils that visually captivated the world around the late 19th and early 20th centuries. Once the austerity brought on by World War I had lifted, the progeny of these scripts evolved into less floriated, though no less flourishy, alphabets. It was at this time, during the early 1920s, that resurgence in graphic and typographic design ran parallel to a surge in the production and promotion of French arts and crafts in various world markets.

Design in general was seen as a postwar national asset, and the French were nothing if not leaders of contemporary, machine-age design. The Art Deco aesthetic—a bridge between older ornamentalism and newer Modernism—was propagated and celebrated in all the *grands magasins* throughout Paris. This graphic design style telegraphed the real and faux extravagances of the era. Script lettering, and all that it symbolized, was integral to the propagation of the commercial message.

What did script symbolize? On one hand, the curlicue-strewn scripts accentuated elegance, as in the masthead for the luscious magazine *La Mode du Jour* (p. 36) or the trademark for Haute Mode (p. 80) buttons. On the other, the more purposely handwritten variations suggested informality, as seen with the sheet music for "Que le temps me dure..." (p. 34). The former underscored the luxe aesthetic so emblematic of high fashion. The latter implied a kind of improvisational jazz-like sensibility.

Yet the real harbinger of the Parisian style, and wellspring for an international design fashion that continued until World War II, was the 1925 Exposition Internationale des Arts Décoratifs et Industriels Modernes along the banks of the Seine. Here, the airbrush was the tool of choice and along with esoteric scripts, streamlined decorative typefaces combined with ziggurats, lightning bolts, sunrays, and stylized undulations.

The 1920s and 1930s also witnessed a period of economic growth that offered new opportunities for manufacturers and merchants. In this milieu, Art Moderne emerged as a ubiquitous Euro-American style. Scripts were not the only shorthand means of signaling the new age, but in France such lettering was frequently used as *écriture de publicité* (advertising script) for cars, aeroplanes, furniture, appliances, and fashion. Even more common was packaging for cosmetics and sundries that was adorned with Deco mannerisms and cursive trademarks and titles.

Not all scripts were, however, linked to the Art Moderne aesthetic. Elegant, steel-engraved cursive letters replete with swirls, ligatures, and shadows created before Art Nouveau were commonly used in printed matter. Influenced by exquisite penmanship, such examples as the *Pages Cahier* (p. 42) cover and the type specimen for Bâtardes Modernes (from Fonderie Typographique de Mayeur, Paris, p. 50) represent the quintessential kinds of social, business, and official script typesetting of the fin de siècle. They continued to be used for hotel and restaurant letter- and billheads years later.

Some native scripts do not easily fit into a specific period style (though they were designed during specific periods). The logo for St. Raphaël apéritif (p. 84), a heavy-fisted brush script with hard-edged ascenders and descenders, is too refined to be ad hoc and yet too rough to be considered elegant. While it has Germanic angularity, it also has a "ribbonesque" appearance found in certain French letters.

The St. Raphaël script is startling, but the most spectacular examples found in France are not on paper or packaging but in the built environment—as glass, wood, and illuminated shop signs. Whatever the rationale for using scripts rather than Roman letters for signs may have been, cursive formed from neon or painted on glass defines the Paris cityscape. The signature red light of La Coupole (which not uncoincidentally looks like a signature), the yellow glow of Les Mouettes, and the white sheen of Le P'tit Saigon (pp. 61–62) are the epitome of French signage and commercial script.

France is a nation of scripts, and Paris is arguably the wellspring of all things cursive. The beauty of the French script is that it is varied in form, while at the same time being unmistakably French. ❧

14

SIMONE MARMY
1928.

Encres Primaires
Laffèche-Bréham
12, Rue de Tournon   **PARIS**

Clichés Mansat & Neuens
33, Rue Hallé   **PARIS**

Papier couché de Marcel Laroche
Dépôt à Paris
44, Rue des Vinaigriers

NÉE   N° 30
Mai 1935

NNEMENTS
(20 Numéros) : Frs 75.

n - Administration - Publicité
e Lafayette — PARIS

Ridendo

Revue gaie pour le Médecin

j'aime qui aime le **BYRRH**

VALENTINE

les belles peintures

En vente chez:

17

"TOUTE LA VILLE EN PARLE" VALNYL *pour décoration mate* - VALENITE *pour un grand brillant.*

Louisette et sa poupée

de M. L. Rossignol

Michel et son jardin

de H. L. Rossignol

ML Rossignol

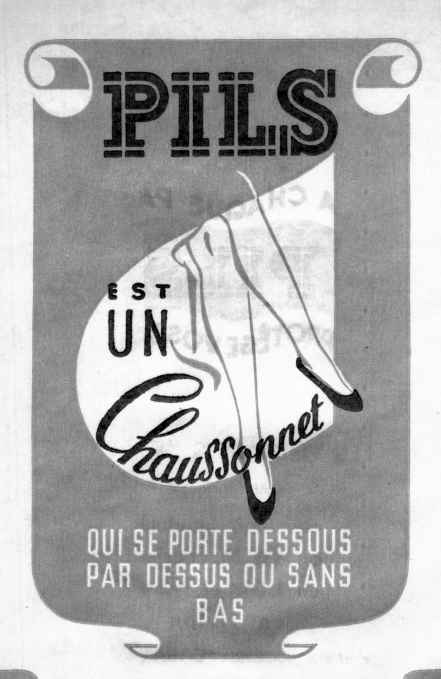

BEURRE CENTRIFUGE

POIDS NET 250 Grammes

Garanti Pur

LES SOUS - VÊTEMENTS

Polichinelle

POUR
**HOMMES
FEMMES
ENFANTS**

PICARDY

Le fidéle reflet de la vigne

Les fameux vins

PICARDY

Le fidéle reflet de la vigne

EST LE PLUS GÉNÉREUX ET LE PLUS FIN DES VINS DE TABLE !

je pénétrai dans le *White City Stadium*.
Le rodéo ne devait commencer que trois
jours plus tard. Quelques cow-boy évo-
luaient sur le pont du navire et plusieurs

rapporteur général.

Elle poursuivra l'examen de ces con-
clusions dans sa prochaine séance.

Toutefois, il reste entendu que pour la

il assurerait dans cette ville,
Mars prochain au tirage de la d...
me tranche de la Loterie Nati...
1936. dans la salle de l'Eldorad...

nerver, grâce
nge de l'œil
d plus opti-
dans lesquels
ne jeune mé-
e Asseline, à
nçaise, uni-
es amis qui,
e de Jacques
conter com-
s incidents.

Acier devait
actives, inté-
entait donc.
avait-il com-
sur les vitres
r une de cel-
os-la forme,
rent impossi-
ce mes agres-
vous de Mme
p. de celle-ci,
le juge d'ins-
lice judiciaire
es investiga-
employé chez
s dont le si-
par les deux
dont la police
Acier et Mme
ent reconnus
ont lancé de
dans l'inté-
é au cabinet
la journée.

, les officiers
te la Légion
re, la Société
oir de Fran-
l'Association
anciens com-
tion des An-
ants Anciens
la Solidarité
nger de No-
ent d'adres-

200.000 Paris

sensibles · *sacrif* · *vente* · *e* · *notre* · *elle* · *commune*

signées vous
...nte aux fins
...nses de la loi
... solution du
...ti « Rouges »
...e Monnet et,
...ont participé
et parlé
...dans la mati-
...le l'agression
...s auxquelles
...actère spon-
...i jour, 13 Fé-
...rmanence de
...l'arrondisse-
...age en règle
...e et dit « Les
...rsions ayant
...au heure qui
...issolution de
...ion française
...tait dans cet
...lle démontre
...doute que si
...de la même
...Association
...t c'est parce
...que ces faits
...re révéler.
...ur donc à ce
...le président
...l y a lieu de,
...les Faucons
...et de leur en
...édition de la
...du 6 Février
...u lendemain
...n Printemps
...des Anciens
...onze heures
...u la relancer
...ie commune
...intervention
...tait dans ses
...nt. L'accusé
...u commerce

24 *Les stylographes français*

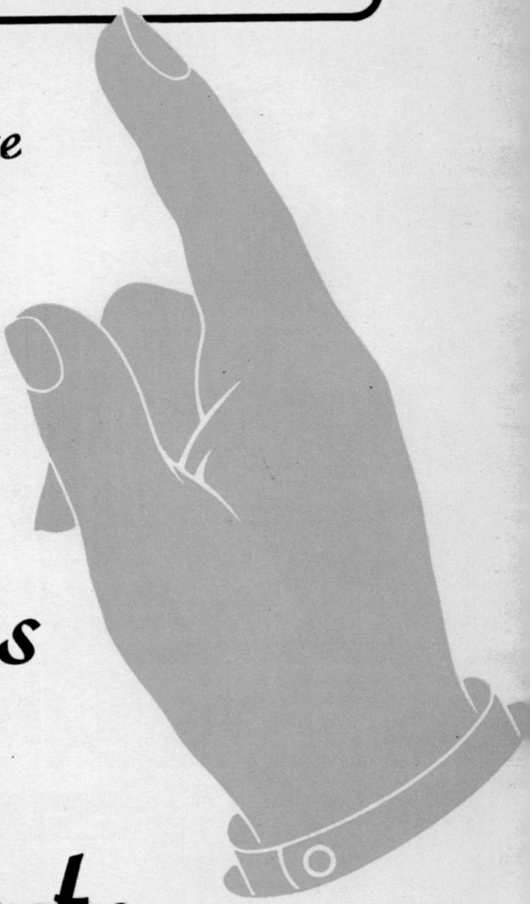

36 *Ronde, gothique et anglaise*

48 *Nouveau caractère*

60 *Rubriques libres*

72 *Bulletins de vote*

84 *Écriture de publicité*

Écriture de publicité virile, et spécifiquement latine, "Scribe" n'est pas un caractère dessiné, c'est une écriture toute naturelle. Elle conserve au texte "écrit" une physionomie familière. Le Scribe est l'"instantané" de l'écriture moderne, fixé par Marcel JACNO

GRAVÉ ET FONDU PAR DEBERNY ET PEIGNOT
18, RUE FERRUS PARIS XIV

8 cicéros

abcdefghijkl

12 cicéros

umnopqrs

20 cicéros

taux

Existe en caractères bois de 8 à 40 cicéros.

"SCRIBE" corps 48

ABCDEFGHIJKLM

NOPQRSTUVXYZ

abcçdefghijklmnopqrsstuvwxyz

12345   .,:;!?""«»   67890

LETTRES A 2 VARIANTES

r ɀ   s s   t t

Le choix entre les 2 variantes est déterminé par le raccord avec la lettre suivante conformément au tableau ci-dessous.

Raccord vers la gauche	Raccord double de milieu	Raccord vers la droite
mer	pari	race
mes	mite	sain
	r de commencement *	
nuit	orme	toge

* Après une lettre ronde ou toute lettre n'offrant aucun raccord vers la droite, il est préférable d'utiliser l'**r** de commencement.

29

Les prénoms effacés

la plus adorable chanson de l'an...

Chanson de Jean Tranchant

CRÉATION DE

Enregistrée sur disque

N° DF 1950

LUCIENNE BOYER
et par Jean TRANCHANT

sur disque PATHÉ" N° PA 963

Mon cœur pleure pour vous

"MY HEART CRIES FOR YOU"

paroles françaises de
LOUIS GASTÉ
paroles anglaises
et musique de
CARL SIGMAN
et
PERCY FAITH

un nouveau grand succès de
Line RENAUD

MASSEY MUSIC COMPANY N.Y.
BEDFORD MUSIC COMPANY N.Y.

la valse que nous dansons

le nouveau grand succès de **André Claveau**

paroles et musique de **Jacques Fuller**

créé et enregistré sur disques Columbia

ÉDITIONS CONTINENTAL

Si Petite

Chanson

Succès de **Lucienne Boyer**

Paroles de
Pierre Bayle

Musique de
Gaston Claret

Prix
6 frs

MÉLODIE FOX

Que le temps me dure...

SŒURS ÉTIENNE
DISQUES DECCA

RADIO 48

Georges GUETARY
PATHE

Studio Harcourt

Graffant

EDITIONS ARPÈGE

PAROLES & MUSIQUE

Vérité-Tango

UN GRAND SUCCES DE

ROBERT RIPA
DISQUE VARIETES
V. 508

PAROLES DE
MAURICE VANDAIR

L'EDITION DES VEDETTES

La Mode du Jour

.1813.   .1814.

En page 7, suite de notre grand Concours des Mariages

(Description
à la page 3)

48ᵉ Année — N° 540   Mars 1933   Prix : 2 fr. 50

JOURNAL DES Ouvrages de Dames

Mon Aiguille

RÉUNIS

François Tedesco
Paris

DÉFINITIONS :

1° — On appelle **corps d'écriture** la hauteur des lettres a, e, u, m, n, etc.

2° — Nous désignerons par **longueur supérieure** ou **inférieure** la longueur dont les lettres bouclées l, b, h, k, respectivement j, y, z dépassent le corps d'écriture.

3° — L'écriture est dite **grosse**, **moyenne** ou **fine** suivant la grandeur du corps d'écriture choisi.

EXEMPLES :
(écrits sur réglure «Seyès»)

«Grosse»	**«Moyenne»**	**«Fine»**
Emploi : grands en-têtes.	Emploi : titres moins importants.	Emploi : écriture courante.
Corps { Papier blanc : 10mm environ d'écriture { Réglure Seyès : 4 interlignes	Corps { Papier blanc : 5mm environ d'écrit. { Réglure Seyès : 2 interlignes	Corps { Papier blanc : 2mm environ d'écriture { Réglure Seyès : 1 interligne
Longueurs sup^re et inf^re : 1 corps 1/2	Longueurs sup^re et inf^re : 2 corps.	Longueurs sup^re et inf^re : 2 corps.

Mêmes PROPORTIONS dans les trois genres d'écriture :

Les lettres :	dépassent le corps d'écriture de :
p et q	3/4 de la longueur inférieure,
d	3/4
t	1/2 } de la longueur supérieure.
p et s	1/4

Mêmes LIGNES DE REPÈRE dans les trois genres d'écriture :

Pour l'exécution des majuscules on dispose de deux lignes de repère principales :

1° — **La médiane** (milieu de la hauteur des majuscules.) Trait : — . — . — (sur le tableau ci-contre.)

2° — **Le milieu du corps d'écriture.** Trait : ....

La boucle initiale des lettres H, I, J, K, Z occupe le dernier 1/3 de la longueur supérieure. Trait : — — —

Les accents et le point de l'i se placent au premier 1/3 de la longueur supérieure. ,

EXEMPLES :

«Grosse»	**«Moyenne»**	**«Fine»**

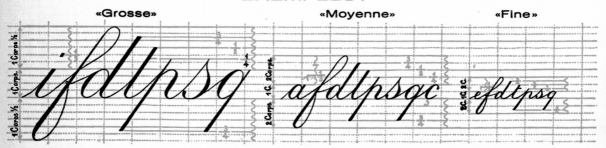

PENTE :

L'écriture peut être droite ou penchée. — Pour cette dernière on obtient la pente en joignant le sommet A du carré ABCD au point E situé au 1/3 du côté CD à partir de C.

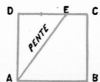

TENUE DU CAHIER :

Pour l'écriture droite le cahier a ses bords parallèles à ceux de la table. — Pour l'écriture penchée on l'incline vers la gauche de manière à ce que la pente forme un angle droit avec le bord de la table.

CONSEIL : {

Commencer par étudier **les formes** en «grosse».
Insister sur l'écriture «moyenne» (la plus souvent employée pour les titres.)
Veiller à **l'application des principes** dans l'écriture «**fine**» courante.

a b c d e f g h i j k l m

n o p q r s t u v w x y z

MEDIANE

Milieu du corps

1/3 supér.

A B C D E F G

H I J K L M N

O P Q R S T U

V W X Y Z

Autre forme de 2: 9

REMARQUE: Pour l'étude, on pourra grouper les lettres par familles:

1 2 3 4 5 6 7 8 9 0

Minuscules:	Chiffres:	Majuscules:
1° i, u, t.	1° 1, 4, 7.	1° A, M, N.
2° n, m, p, v, w, r.	2° 0, 6, 9, 8.	2° P, B, R, F.
3° c, o, a, d, q.	3° 2, 3, 5.	3° S, L, D.
4° e, x, s.		4° U, V, W, Y.
5° l, b, f, h, k.		5° I, J, H, K.
6° j, g, y, z.		6° O, C, G, E, T.
		7° 2, X, Z.

Modèle d'écriture Bléger.

Tous droits réservé — Prix de la feuille : 60 centimes.
Feuille 1: Cursive. — Feuille 2: Ronde et Bâtarde normalisées.
Feuille 3 : Ecriture ton normalisée et écritures décoratives.

Editées par C. Bléger, Professeur d'E.P.S.
3, rue St-Ar[...]

Chèques

Cornil-Delar...

-Cahors-

(France)

La plaque Électrolytique

VIVOL

Grâce à l'application du principe de l'Électrolyse aux travaux ménagers, en employant **VIVOL**, votre argenterie sera toujours neuve.

VIVOL est garanti n'attaquant pas le métal et nettoie sans user Ruolz, Argent, Or, Platine, contr...

120

Pages

N° 51

Cahier de

Comedies

APPARTENANT A Claire Paudrelier

DEMEURANT A Sevres 8 Av. de Bellevue (S.&.

42

Galeries Lafayette Paris

PARFUMERIE SAVONNERIE

SAVON SURFIN

Eau de Cologn

TRIPLE EXTRAIT

Paris

Lynette
LINGERIE PARFAITE

TOMOX

PRODUIT
LIEBIG

CONSOMMÉ
AUX EXTRAITS DE VIANDE,
CONCENTRÉS DE TOMATES
CONTENU: ET EXTRAITS VÉGÉTAUX. 250 Gr.
DÉPÔT GÉNÉRAL DES PRODUITS LIEBIG, S. A. ANVERS

Un nouveau produit Liebig

CARACTÈRES
ORDINAIRES
& DE FANTAISIE
ORNÉS & FILETÉS
MODERNES
& CLASSIQUES
ÉCRITURE PARISIENNE
ANGLAISES
BATARDES, RONDES
& GOTHIQUES

INTERLIGNES
EN LAMES
ET SYSTÉMATIQUES

ACCOLADES

VIGNETTES
ORNEMENTS
GENRE NOUVEAU
& FILETS ORNÉS

GALVANOPLASTIE
MÉDAILLES
PASSE-PARTOUT
POUR
CARTES DE COMMERCE
ET
TÊTES DE PAGES
ATTRIBUTS
SUJETS POUR MENUS

AFFICHES

M

Dernièrement en vous soumettant nos

Trois Collections d'Ornements Japonais

nous avons annoncé la présentation prochaine

des modèles d'emploi tirés de chaque collection.

Aujourd'hui nous avons le plaisir de don-

ner, dans les pages suivantes, des Compositions

faites avec les pièces de la Première Collection

exclusivement.

Vous remarquerez certainement le parti qu'en

peuvent tirer les typographes chargés de vos Travaux

de ville & Annonces

Dans l'espoir d'être favorisés de vos ordres,

nous vous prions d'agréer, Monsieur, nos bien

sincères salutations

Allainguillaume & Cⁱᵉ

Caractères d'écriture

Corps 16 — Le kil. 9 fr. 50 — Min. 6 kil.

Nous vous remercions de l'excellent accueil que vous avez bien voulu réserver à notre Représentant lors de la visite qu'il vous a faite, ainsi que de l'importante commande de caractères et de filets systématiques que vous lui avez remise. Nous la notons avec soin et vous en ferons l'expédition le plus tôt possible, en tenant compte de toutes les indications et instructions que vous lui avez données à ce sujet.

Dans l'espoir que vous aurez entière satisfaction de notre envoi, nous vous prions d'agréer, Monsieur, nos salutations les plus empressées.

Corps 22 — Le kil. 7 fr. — Min 8 kil.

J'ai reçu, Monsieur, votre nouveau livre contre le genre humain et je vous en remercie. Vous plairez aux hommes, à qui vous dites toute la vérité; mais vous ne les corrigerez pas. On ne peut peindre avec des couleurs plus fortes les horreurs de la Société moderne, dont notre ignorance et notre faiblesse se promettent tant de douces mais combien vaines consolations.

Espérant que vous ne faillirez point à la tâche que vous vous êtes imposée, soyez assuré, cher Monsieur, de ma profonde sympathie.

47

Ecriture Parisienne

Nº 9099. — Corps 9

Nous avons l'honneur de vous informer que nous mettons en vente actuellement un lot important de Marchandises en Solde, qui constituent des Occasions uniques. Nous vous engageons donc vivement à visiter nos Galeries, où vous trouverez assurément à faire votre choix dans de bonnes conditions. Exposition du Mobilier le 7 Octobre 1924

Nº 9100. — Corps 12

Les efforts constants et les soins que nous apportons dans l'exécution des commandes, nous permettent de garantir nos appareils. La bonne renommée de notre Maison est la meilleure référence sur la qualité de nos fournitures Assemblée des Sociétés de Secours Mutuels, à Paris, le 25 Février 1925

Nº 9101. — Corps 16

Nous avons eu la bonne fortune de découvrir dernièrement à Venise un portrait original de Casanova de Seingalt, en l'an 1760, à l'âge même où il écrivit ses intéressants Mémoires, notre collaborateur André Baschet en a prouvé l'authenticité

Nº 9102. — Corps 20

Sans entrer dans les détails historiques, nous allons examiner les séries de lettres ornées dont nous trouvons les spécimens divers dans les impressions La Fonderie Typographique Française, à Paris

Nº 9103. — Corps 24 (Petit œil)

Plantes d'ornementation et Garnitures pour grands galas Cours d'Horticulture, 24, rue de Paradis

Nº 9104. — Corps 24 (Gros œil)

Grande Exposition de Tableaux de Peinture le 30 Avril 1924, Salle Drouot

Mr & Mme Langlois

Verdun

Benjamin Jacquelin

Avocat à la Cour d'Appel

25, Rue Saint-Jean, Caen

Mademoiselle Elise Barolan

Écriture Parisienne
Corps (24 2 œils) 15 fr. le Kilo
Corps 12 : 20 fr. le Kilo

Paris, le 15 Décembre 1904

Nous avons l'honneur de vous présenter ce Caractère nouveau, très lisible, pouvant servir à la composition de vos Circulaires, Manchettes, Réclames, Traites & travaux soignés

Ce genre d'écriture a son emploi tout indiqué pour les Cartes de Visite modernes. La gravure comprendra les corps 9, 12, 16, 20 & 24 (ce dernier, 2 œils)

Dans l'espoir que vous voudrez bien nous favoriser de vos ordres, nous vous prions d'agréer, Monsieur, nos bien sincères salutations

Allainguillaume & Cie

Graveurs-Fondeurs   21, Rue du Montparnasse

L'emploi de ces Caractères pour Circulaires & tous Travaux Modernes est recommandé

Bâtardes Modernes

Corps 12 — 16 fr. le kilo — Minim. 3 kil.

États Généraux de 1793	Boulevard Magenta, 28
Marion Delorme	Seine-&-Oise
Vélo-Club de Saint-Etienne	Compagnie Française du Gaz

Corps 16 — 15 fr. le kilo — Minim. 4 kil.

Société Anonyme avec Personnel & Capital variables
Excursions aux Sables-d'Olonne

Corps 20 — 14 fr. le kilo — Minim. 5 kil.

Voyages Circulaires aux Plages de l'Océan
Fêtes du Carnaval de Nice

Corps 24 — 12 fr. le kilo — Minim. 6 kil.

Imprimeries Typo - Lithographiques
Grand Prix d'Honneur

Corps 30 — 11 fr. le kilo — Minim. 8 kil.

Prise de Saint - Jean - d'Acre
Union Républicaine

Ces Bâtardes Modernes s'alignent sur les Corps correspondants des Écritures Bâtardes maigres & grasses
(Voir à la page suivante les Essais de Composition de ces divers corps)

1

Gaston Berthier

35, Rue du Louvre

20

Madame Vernon

2

Mademoiselle Brémontier

Professeur de Mandoline

34, Rue du Louvre

3

Claudius Guillermin

Instituteur

Montluçon

4

Eugène Reymond

Trésorier-Payeur Général du département de la Charente

ANGOULÊME

5

Emile Herbelot

Professeur d'Anglais au Lycée Charlemagne

5, Rue Bleue

6

Charles Grandier

Négociant

MONTMIRAIL

7

Honoré Richard

Publiciste

BORDEAUX

8

Madame Léon Verchère

MARDI

9

Benjamin Franklin

COMPIÈGNE

Bordeaux, le _____ 1895   **BPF.**

Le _____ veuillez payer contre ce Mandat à votre ordre

la somme de _____

valeur en Marchandises suivant _____ avis du

N° |

Rue Sainte-Catherine, 45

TIMBRE MOBILE

Dunkerque, le _____ 1895   **BPF.**

A _____ veuillez payer contre ce Mandat

à ordre

de _____ la somme

valeur reçue en Marchandises que payerez suivants avis.

BPF M.

TIMBRE MOBILE

Renée

N° 0

Paraphes en Cuivre pour Signatures

Emile Girardin

N° 1

Pierre Corneille

N° 2

André Maulde

N° 3

Prix de chaque Paraphe : 2 FRANCS

Nous pouvons fournir dans cette forme des paraphes plus grands à des prix variant suivant la longueur

Fonderie Allainguillaume & Cie, Successeurs de Mayeur, à Paris

10 a 5 A 2299 - c. 48 10 k. 30

La lumière du soleil,
brisée et amortie

15 a 8 A 2298 - c. 36 8 k. 30

Après le souper, on veille
Encore deux heures

15 a 8 A 2297 - c. 28 5 k. 20

Moi, pauvre malheureux, réduit
aux simples ressources de
257 la Nature 384

30 a 10 A 2296 - c. 24 6 k. 20

Peu d'existences furent plus fortunées
que celle du Titien, le brillant
chef de l'école vénitienne. Les

5 a 2 A   12518 - c. 72   13 k. 40

Eden - Palace

5 a 2 A   12517 - c. 60   10 k. 20

Hôtel du Midi

8 a 3 A   12516 - c. 48   8 k. 60

Banque de France

8 a 3 A   12519 - c. 42   6 k. 80

Compagnies Maritimes

Les quatre corps s'alignent en pied

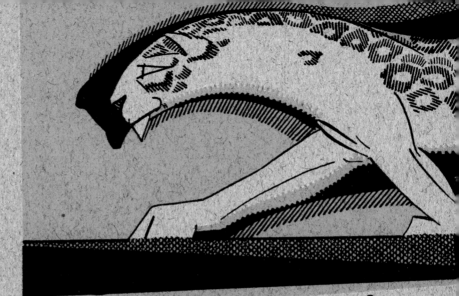

La Beauté de l'Impr

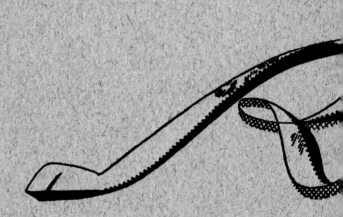

LOUIS MULLER
PARIS

Papiers

né sur couverture série "Ruskin Bristol", Coffée, n° 4701 en 58 × 78 des ...eries LOUIS MULLER & FILS, Paris.

Couleurs de
CH. LORILLEUX
& Cⁱᵉ

Dessin créé et exécuté dans les Ateliers de
CHANLOUP, Paris.
Imprimé par les Cours professionnels
5, rue Séguier, Paris.

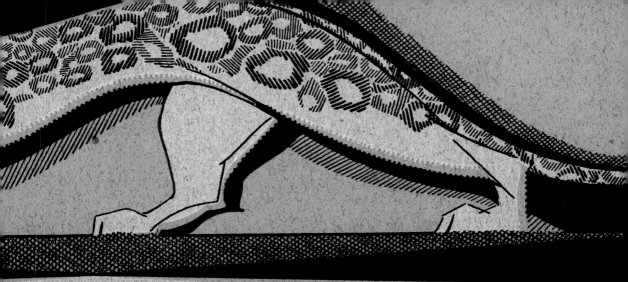

...cion par la qualité du papie...

FILS
...our Couvertures
DE GRAND LUXE

TABAC

TABAC

Tabac

Les Mouettes

Les Mouettes

SALON DE THE

Le Select

Le Petit Lutetia

Le P'tit Saigon

Le Train de Vie

Restauration, Salon
delicatessen

de l'Hôtel d

Le Feuille-Thé

Le Montana

LUNCH-DINER-JAZZ

SAVON FIN

jardin fleuri

VIOLETTE
COSMYDOR
PARIS

SAVON FIN

jardin fleuri

JASMIN

COSMYDOR

PARIS

Menthe

Nº 100 DEROSE

DÉPOSÉ

Alcool

Brûler

NATURÉ

L.C.

PARIS

JUS DE RAISIN

CHALLAND

ALIMENT DE RÉGIME
Plus riche que le lait
ASSIMILABILITÉ PARFAITE

réalise la *Cure de Raisin* en toutes saisons, nourrit et soutient le malade sans introduire aucune substance toxique azote ou chlorure

LITTÉRATURE et ÉCHANTILLONS   **JUS DE RAISIN CHALLAND**   **NUITS-St-GEORGES (Côte d'Or)**

Garanti pur

Savon
Eau de Cologne
Extra fin

Garanti pur

CHARME DISCRET
ACINTHE MAUVE

Les Eaux de
Lotions surfine

Eau de fleurs d'oranger

DÉPOSÉ N° 367

MOSAIQUE BY

Initiale

Cologne fleuries
pour la Chevelure

JONQUILLE D

SANKAR

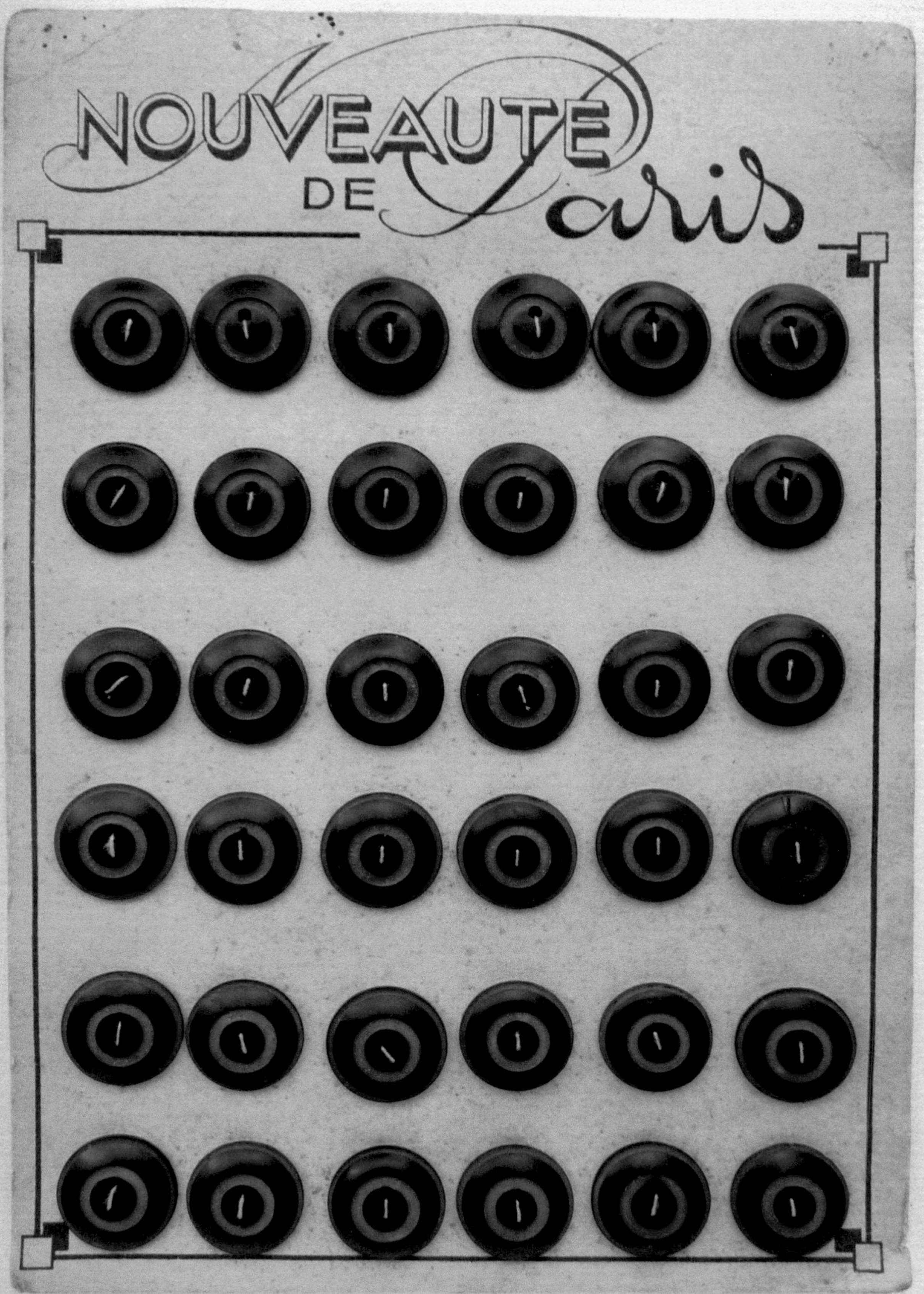
NOUVEAUTE
DE Paris

haute Mode

N FRANCE   R.F

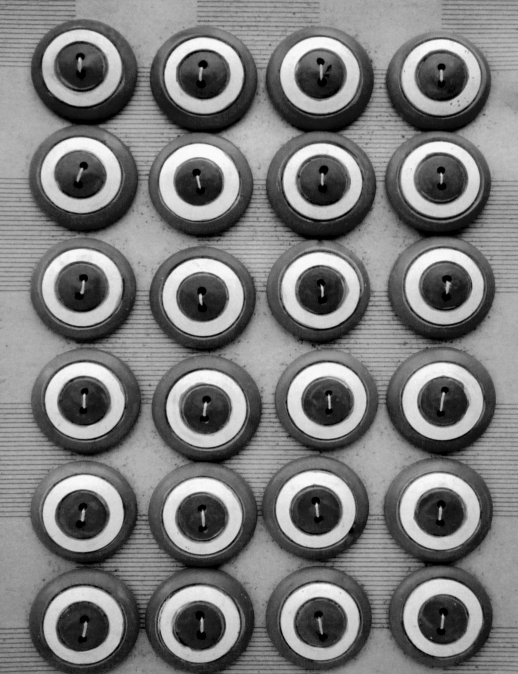

Grande mode

FABRICATION FRANÇAISE

81

La Mode

Déposé

83

inquina

S.A.S.A.G.O.

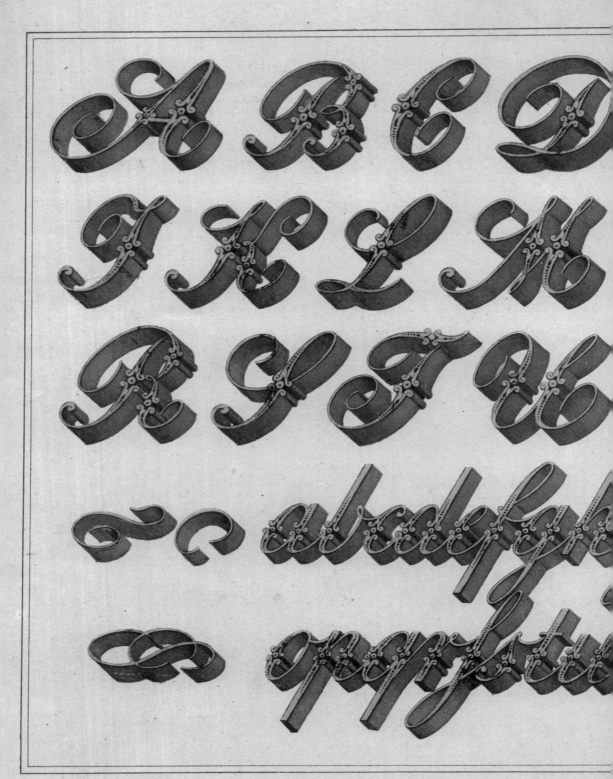

Vᵉ A. MOREL & Cⁱᵉ Éditeurs

Girault Sculp.

Imp. LEMERCIER r de Seine 57 Paris

14–15. Typographic specimen sheet from Paul Marmy, Paris, 1928.

16. Customized script for *Ridendo*, a medical revue, Paris, 1935.

17. Handwriting script for Byrrh liquor, *c.* 1930; script for logo of Valentine paints, *c.* 1930.

18–19. Hand-lettered script for children's books by M. L. Rossignol, 1932.

20. Hand-lettered script for Pils hosiery packaging, 1937.

21. Hand-lettered script for Centrifuge butter packaging, 1928.

22. Trademark for Polichinelle underwear, *c.* 1930.

23. Hand-lettered script for Picardy wine advertisement, *c.* 1940.

24–25. Brush script for Printemps department store, newspaper advertisement, 1953.

26–27. Jacno script specimen sheet, designed by Marcel Jacno for Fonderies Deberny et Peignot, date unknown.

28–29. Scribe Script specimen sheet from Fonderies Deberny et Peignot, date unknown.

30. Hand-lettered script for "Les prénoms éffacés" song sheet, *c.* 1950.

31. Hand-lettered script for "Mon cœur pleure pour vous" song sheet, *c.* 1950.

32. Hand-lettered script for "La valse que nous dansons" song sheet, *c.* 1940.

33. Hand-lettered script for "Si petite" song sheet, *c.* 1940.

34. Hand-lettered script for "Que le temps me dure . . ." song sheet, *c.* 1950.

35. Hand-lettered script for "Vérité-tango" song sheet, *c.* 1950.

36. Masthead for *La Mode du Jour* magazine, 1933.

37. Masthead for *Journal des Ouvrages des Dames*, 1933.

38–39. Manual for cursive handwriting, 1931.

40–41. Various labels for canned fruit, silver polish, and a clothing shop, *c.* 1928.

42. Cover of a notebook, *c.* 1925.

43. Wrapping paper with logo for Galeries Lafayette, Paris, *c.* 1935.

44–45. Label for Savon Surfin eau de Cologne and Lynette lingerie (left); advertisement for Tomox consommé (right), 1930–35.

46–47. Specimen pages from "Collections d'ornements japonais" in the Fonderie Typographique de Mayeur, Paris (left), and "Caractères d'écriture" in the Fonderie Typographique Française, Paris, catalogs, *c.* 1923.

48–49. Specimen pages from Écriture Parisienne in the Fonderie Typographique Française, Paris, catalog, *c.* 1923.

50–51. Specimen pages from Bâtardes Modernes in the Fonderie Typographique Française, Paris, catalogs, *c.* 1923.

52. Bank cheques from Bordeaux and Dunkerque, 1895.

53. Specimen of copper engravings for signatures in Fonderie Typographique de Mayeur, Paris, catalog, *c.* 1921.

54–55. Airbrushed script for point-of-sale displays, *c.* 1928.

56–57. Specimen pages for Médicis (left) and Lithographiques (right) in the Fonderies Deberny et Peignot, catalog, Paris, *c.* 1925.

58–59. Advertisement for Louis Muller et Fils, Paris, paper company, 1928.

60. Logo for Gevaert film, 1940s.

61–63. Various neon, plastic, and painted signs in Paris (photographs by Louise Fili).

64–65. Page from lettering manual, *La Lettre Artistique & Moderne* by Draim, 1932.

66–67. Packaging for Jardin Fleuri soap, *c.* 1930.

68–69. Various labels for soaps and fragrances, 1920s.

70–71. Label for denatured alcohol, Alcool à Brûler, 1924.

72. Hand-lettered script advertisement for Jus de Raisin, health tonic, date unknown.

73. Wrapper for eau de Cologne soap, *c.* 1927.

74–75. Point-of-sale (easel-back) display for L' Initiale eau de Cologne and label for orange-flower cologne, 1920s.

76–77. Hanging three-dimensional display sign for Briottet crème de cassis, 1945.

78–79. Hand-lettered script button cards for Haute Couture and Nouveauté de Paris (brands), 1930s.

80–81. Hand-lettered script button cards for fashion brands Haute Mode and Grande Mode, 1930s.

82–83. Hand-lettered script button cards for fashion brands Haute Nouveauté and La Mode, 1930s.

84–85. Logo for St. Raphaël apéritif on enamel sign, 1950.

86–87. Specimen letters for sign painters by Le Mercier, Paris, *c.* 1928.

British

OLD ENGLISH IS ARGUABLY ONE OF THE MOST RECOGNIZ-ABLE VINTAGE BLACK LETTER DESIGNS IN THE WORLD of typography. And just as King George V of England and Kaiser Wilhelm II of Germany were related by blood, this engraved typeface is a kissing-close cousin of the German Fraktur type. Fraktur, from the Latin *fractum*, means "broken script." So, technically Old English is a script, though it is not exactly cursive and the letters are more or less separate without connective tissue. Nonetheless, it is considered a script, though not the sole English variety.

Another cursive style—Secretary Hand—was widely used as hand-writing in England from the early 16th century onward for both personal correspondence and official documents. However, this too was not always joined together. The "fair hand," the standardized script for business and social documents, developed during the 19th century and established itself in Britain (and later the United States).

Authentic English scripts—not those readymade imports from France, like Parisian Ronde (p. 92), which was made available through the leading English type foundry, Stephenson Blake & Co. Ltd, but rather Imperial Script (p. 93), made by the same foundry—have regal connotations. Just listen to this: "We have much pleasure in calling attention to the Imperial Script," states the promotional text in the specimen sheet, dated 1935. "The popularity of this series is already quite phenomenal, and is due not only to its elegant appearance, but also to its durable qualities." Sounds like the queen herself is making the claim. It continues, "This series is cast on sloping bodies, and as there are no overhanging sorts, is thus free from an objection usually inherent in scripts." Then, with perfect imperious elocution the text concludes: "The utmost care has been taken to ensure accurate junctions, and in this respect also the series claims to be superior to most other scripts." Such grandeur.

The English have always taken their scripts quite seriously. Look at Stephenson Blake's Palace Script (p. 94), the companion series "to the world-renowned 'Society Script' with the qualities of Copperplate Engraving." These are the scripts that put the swoosh and swash into the royal family of scripts.

Yet from a typographic angle, British type was not about elegance alone. Britain was also the birthplace of the Industrial Revolution, and since it was just as wrapped up in commerce as any other industrial nation, many commercial scripts were at its printers' disposal. Not all British alphabets, however, were designed with the same élan as the royal collections. The unceremoniously titled Light Script (p. 96) and Heavy Script (p. 97) were definite advertising workhorses. Likewise, in Ariston Light and Medium (p. 99) there are eye-catching quirks where the capitals and lower cases join, but the suggestion of aristocracy in the title is overstated. Similarly, Temple Script (p. 100) has a delightful cursive motion, but it is intended to communicate notices in a newspaper, not messages on a high-society calling card.

The best-known British scripts are those calligraphic numbers used as bookplates and other personal identifiers (pp. 104–7). Popular in the late 19th and early 20th centuries, they are routinely white on black, placed in ovals or squares and filled with an excessive amount of filigree framing the name or initials of the "branded" individual. The craft necessary to ensure that the thicks and thins do not get lost amid the black involves considerable practice. These are the models for many of the pastiches created for the "olde-worlde" kinds of sundry or food products that are designed to look as though they have a heritage and to conjure nostalgic longing among customers. Scripts have a way of triggering memory.

Perhaps the most glorious of all this country's scripts are for signs. Achieving the skill to execute a perfect script-signature on a glass shop-front using hands, paint, mahl sticks and pounce wheels does not happen overnight: it takes years of arduous apprenticeship to be a successful sign painter. And not all sign painters truly master the script. Compare the logo for Lillywhites of London to that for Fenwick (p. 111) and consider which artisan has better captured and controlled the fluid line. ❧

48 Point   2 A, 8 a; about 10½ lb.

London Establishments
Création Parisienne

36 Point   3 A, 16 a; about 9½ lb.

Handsome Series for Invitations
Cards and Social Stationery

30 Point   4 A, 20 a; about 9 lb.

Fashionable Milliner visits Irish Capital
Innovation in Headwear from Paris

24 Point   5 A, 34 a; about 9 lb.

Printers who desire to obtain Copperplate Effects
will find Parisian Ronde an ideal letter

18 Point   7 A, 64 a; about 9 lb.

Musical Entertainment attracts numerous audiences from
surrounding neighbourhood during month of June

14 Point   7 A, 64 a; about 6 lb.

Parisian Ronde may be appropriately used for Dainty Circulars, Menus
and Admission Cards, Wedding Invitations, and Personal Stationery

The following special sorts are included in all founts:

.... d r r. rs. o'c o (, , , , , ,

2557

Imperial Script

We have much pleasure in calling attention to the Imperial Script. The popularity of this series is already quite phenomenal, and is due not only to its elegant appearance, but also to its durable qualities. The series is cast on sloping bodies, and, as there are no overhanging sorts, is thus free from an objection usually inherent in scripts. The utmost care has been taken to ensure accurate junctions, and in this respect also the series claims to be superior to most other scripts. The Dotted Lines................which are included in each fount, will be found both useful and economical as regards time and labour.

Stephenson, Blake & Co. Ltd.

Sheffield & London

Palace Script

Companion series to the world-renowned
Society Script with the qualities
of Copperplate Engraving

Designed and Engraved by
Stephenson, Blake & Co. Limited
The Letter Foundry, Sheffield
London and Manchester

PALACE SCRIPT

CAST ON SLOPING BODIES

36 Point   2 A, 14 a ; about 11 lb.

Kensington Symphony Orchestra
Entrancing Musical Introduction

30 Point   3 A, 16 a ; about 9 lb.

Handsome Script for careful Printer
Recommended by Eminent Journalist

24 Point   4 A, 24 a ; about 8½ lb.

Opening Ceremony of the Royal Docks
Patagonian Iron Development Company
Belgian Philanthropist donates £234567

18 Point   6 A, 40 a ; about 7 lb.

The accuracy of form and mechanical perfection of
Palace, Society and Imperial Scripts are among the
greatest triumphs of the art of the letter founder

Stephenson, Blake & Co. Ltd.
The Letter Foundry, Sheffield
London and Manchester

Light Script

Series 351. 36 Point   14 lbs. A 6 a 16

Modern Commercial Pract 123

Series 351. 30 Point   7 lbs. A 4 a 13

Modern Commercial Practice is 1234

Series 351. 24 Point   7 lbs. A 7 a 19

Modern Commercial Practice is hereafter 123456

Series 351. 18 Point   7 lbs. A 15 a 37

Modern Commercial Practice is hereafter symbolised 12345678

Series 351. 14 Point   7 lbs. A 26 a 67

Modern Commercial Practice is hereafter symbolised by the charac 1234567890

Formal Script

Series 436. 18 Point   7 lbs. A 18 a 42

Modern Commercial Practice is hereafter symbolised by the characteristics of up-to-date printers' type. Nevertheless the very type faces, most in use to-day, were designed by craftsmen who were the contemporaries of Benjamin Huntsman. In our knowledge and use of the   1234567890

Grosvenor Script

Series 493. 18 Point   7 lbs. A 15 a 35

Modern Commercial Practice is hereafter symbolised by the characteristics of up-to-date printers' type. Nevertheless the very type faces,   1234567890

Script Series 475

Series 475. 24 Point   7 lbs. A 8 a 18

Modern Commercial Practice is hereafter symbolised by the characteristics of up-to-date   1234567890

[154]

Series 322. 72 Point   28 lbs. A 4 a 9

Modern Co 123

Series 322. 60 Point   28 lbs. A 6 a 14

Modern Com 123

Series 322. 48 Point   14 lbs. A 4 a 9

Modern Commerc 123

Series 322. 42 Point   14 lbs. A 6 a 14

Modern Commercial 123

Series 322. 36 Point   14 lbs. A 9 a 18

Modern Commercial Pr 1234

Series 322. 30 Point   7 lbs. A 6 a 14

Modern Commer-cial Pract 12345

Series 322. 24 Point   7 lbs. A 7 a 15

Modern Commercial Practice is 123456

Series 322. 18 Point   7 lbs. A 12 a 27

Modern Commercial Practice is hereafter symbolised by the characteristics of 12345678

Series 322. 14 Point   7 lbs. A 21 a 46

Modern Commercial Practice is here-after symbolised by the characteristics of up-to-date print 1234567890

[153]

97

Tyres by Dunlop

C.F.H.64

no. 584 187   12 point
15×A   45×a   17×1   1 fount about 4 lbs.

Our "Ariston" Series reflects elegance and harmony

no. 584 198   12 point
14×A   40×a   15×1   1 fount about 4 lbs.

Our famous Books are Gifts of great distinction

no. 584 188   14 point small
12×A   57×a   15×1   1 fount about 4,75 lbs.

A Master Script for modern advertisements

no. 584 199   14 point small
12×A   52×a   12×1   1 fount about 4,75 lbs.

A musical Instrument of great quality

no. 584 189   14 point large
10×A   22×a   12×1   1 fount about 4,75 lbs.

Scotch Whiskies since the year 1897

no. 584 200   14 point large
9×A   24×a   11×1   1 fount about 4,75 lbs.

The Art Institute of Liverpool

no. 584 190   18 point
8×A   24×a   11×1   1 fount about 5,25 lbs.

Gems of many colours and sizes

no. 584 201   18 point
8×A   18×a   10×1   1 fount about 5,25 lbs.

Clothes to wear on Sailboats

no. 584 191   24 point small
6×A   16×a   10×1   1 fount about 6,5 lbs.

We have some new ideas

no. 584 202   24 point small
6×A   12×a   9×1   1 fount about 6,5 lbs.

Yachting on the River

no. 584 192   24 point large
5×A   14×a   9×1   1 fount about 6,5 lbs.

The modern creations

no. 584 203   24 point large
5×A   11×a   8×1   1 fount about 6,5 lbs.

Produce of Canada

no. 584 193   30 point
4×A   10×a   7×1   1 fount about 8 lbs.

Comforts of home

no. 584 204   30 point
4×A   9×a   7×1   1 fount about 8 lbs.

Western United

no. 584 194   36 point
3×A   8×a   5×1   1 fount about 9,75 lbs.

Picture Book

no. 584 205   36 point
3×A   7×a   5×1   1 fount about 11 lbs.

Model Toys

no. 584 195   48 point
3×A   6×a   5×1   1 fount about 14 lbs.

New Stars

no. 584 206   48 point
3×A   6×a   5×1   1 fount about 16 lbs.

Old Spice

no. 584 207   60 point
3×A   6×a   4×1   1 fount about 23 lbs.

Airport

The book letter used in this specimen is WALBAUM and WALBAUM ITALIC, one of the finest
classic characters in the world, a product of the Berthold Type Foundry, Berlin/Germany.

This face is also available in 60 and 72 point

Series 455.   48 Point   14 lbs. A 4 a 8

Commercial Prac 123

Series 455.   36 Point   14 lbs. A 7 a 15

Modern Commercial P 1234

Series 455.   .30 Point   7 lbs. A 5 a 10

Modern Commercial Practice 12345

Carpets _____

of Quality and Distinction

_____

from
Allen & Son's Carpet Warehouse

Series 455.   24 Point (Large Face)   7 lbs. A 7 a 16

Modern Commercial Practice is here 123456

Series 455.   24 Point (Small Face)   7 lbs. A 8 a 24

Modern Commercial Practice is hereafter 123456

Series 455.   18 Point   7 lbs. A 21 a 49

Modern Commercial Practice is hereafter symbolised by the characteristics of up-to-date printers' type.   Nevertheless the very type faces 123456

Series 455.   12 Point   7 lbs. A 28 a 74

Modern Commercial Practice is hereafter symbolised by the characteristics of up-to-date printers' type. Nevertheless the very type faces, most in use to-day, were designed by craftsmen who were 123456

[152]

A B C D E F G H I J K
L M N O P Q R S T U
V W X Y Z abcdefghijklmn
opqrstuvwxyz 1234567890½ "nd

A B C D E F G H I J K Lmnopqrstuvwxyzr¼ M¿æ&¿ "nd th st   14

A B C D E F G H I Jklmnopqrstuvwxyzabcde   18

F G H I J Klmnopqrstuvwx   30

X Y Z Abcdefghijklmn   36

Sizes available: 14, 18, 24, 30, 36pt.

W. S. Cowell Ltd, Ipswich, Suffolk

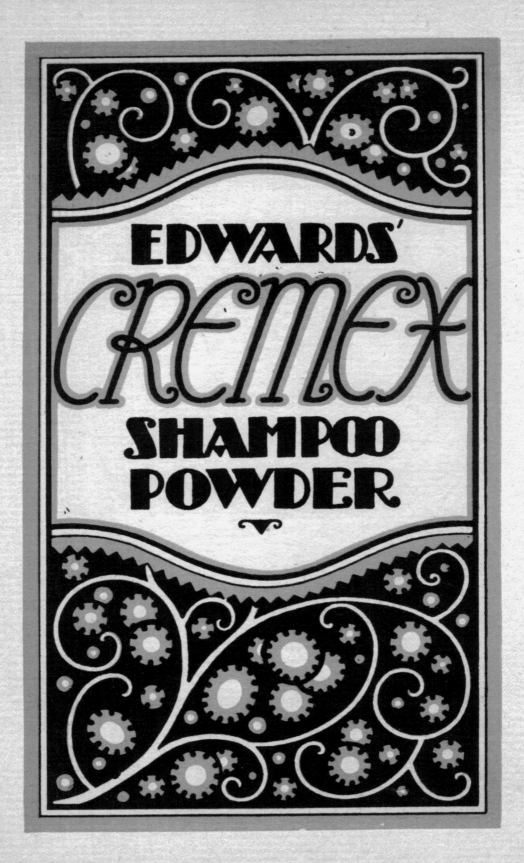

Dorothy
Perkins
& Others

VOGUE

Somewhere
in Sussex

Philip Furneaux Jordan

Violet Ashby

Nancy Tennant

Irene Murray Hyslop

Katherine & Lance Thirkell

SCRIBNERS of New York
are always ready to purchase
FIRST EDITIONS
and RARE BOOKS
in fine condition for cash
23 Bedford Square London WC1

Audrey Cheshire

The History of
Hyde Park
and
The House of
The Grosvenors
by
Sir Max Pemberton

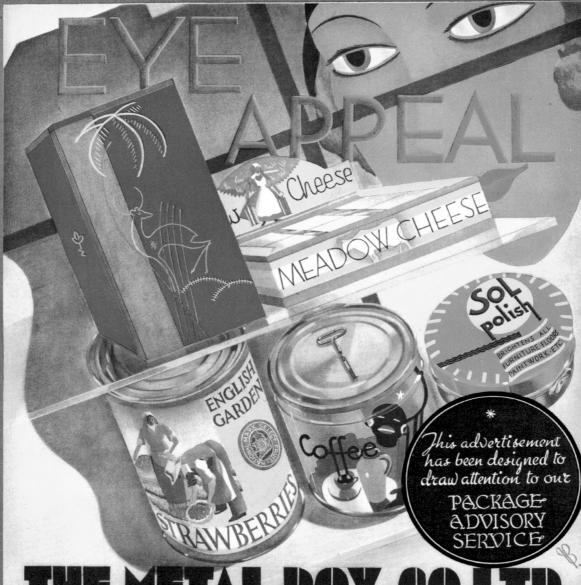

Directions for Learn...

The proportion of Letters is regul...
by the O & N; therefore practise them first
in a large Character.

Make All Your Body-Strokes with
the Full, & all Hair-Strokes with the
corner of Your Pen.

Never turn Your Pen, nor alter the
Position of Your hand.

Let Your hair-Strokes be proportion'd
to Your Body-Strokes & answer one another.

Your Letters without Stems must be
even at top & bottom.

Let Your Stems above be equal in
length to l (t only excepted)

Your Stems below must be equal in
length to j.

Let Your Capitals be equal in height

92–93. Specimen of Parisian Ronde (left) and Imperial Script (right) from Stephenson Blake & Co. catalog, 1935.

94–95. Specimen of Palace Script from Stephenson Blake & Co. catalog, 1935.

96–97. Specimen of Light Script and Heavy Script from Stephenson Blake & Co. catalog, 1945.

98. Magazine advertisement for Dunlop tyres in *Punch* using a version of Palace Script, 1928.

99. Specimens of Ariston Light and Ariston Medium from an unknown foundry, influenced by the Berthold Foundry, Berlin, *c.* 1930.

100–1. Specimen of Temple Script (left) from an unknown foundry and Marian Script (right) from W. S. Cowell Ltd.

102. Hand-lettered script for Cremex dry shampoo label by Alfred Erdmann, *c.* 1928.

103. Various script drawings from a lettering manual, *c.* 1928.

104–7. Various script type treatments by Reynolds Stone used for bookplates, etc., 1930s.

108. Hand-lettered brand name for special paper stock from the Clyde Paper Co., Scotland, 1940s.

109. Script title for *The History of Hyde Park* book cover, 1937.

110. Headline for the packaging section of *Advertising Display* magazine, 1932.

111. Brand logo for Lillywhites department store, London, *c.* 1938.

111. Shop sign on glass for Fenwick of London, date unknown.

112. Part of the 'Directions for Learners' from an engraved copybook, 1887.

German

THE ORNATE SPECIMEN SHEET REPRODUCED IN THIS SECTION, TITLED MODERNE SCHRIFTEN, IS NOT THE only popular cursive style to emerge from Germany between the two world wars (pp. 116–17). However, it was one of the most emblematic of the world's national lettering styles. During the Third Reich it was called *Volksschrift* (people's lettering) and politicized in aggressive ways.

Moderne Schriften is a customized Black Letter or Fraktur, the primary Germanic style that was used for printed and written materials from the 16th century until 1940. After this date the fickle Nazi officials deemed it ideologically questionable and dangerously illegible. Fraktur is a "broken script," so called because its sharply defined, ornamental curlicues break the continuous line of a word. It is also called Deutsche Schrift, and before its fall from political grace it was promoted by Nazi cultural organizations as the quintessential Aryan script. Pageants and contests were organized throughout Germany to identify the perfect writers—good Germans all.

Gothic Minuscule, a Black Letter script, was used in western Europe until the 17th century, when Latin was adopted. Fraktur, a collective singular noun when it refers to a typeface or handwriting, came in very many font variations and was the official lettering style for government and ecclesiastical documents dating back to Johannes Gutenberg and the invention of printing in the 15th century. But for everyday writing Sütterlin was the script of choice. Created by the Berlin designer L. Sütterlin (1865–1917), it was modeled on a style of handwriting used in the old German chancery. The spiky handwriting, angularly reminiscent of the marks on a polygraph or electro-cardiograph printout, was taught in German schools from 1915 to 1941 and is still used by elderly Germans. Legibility was always a real challenge.

Although certain "un-German" typefaces were banned by the state under the Nazi regime, most type foundries throughout Germany produced a large number of non-Fraktur script faces based on Latin lettering and known as Antiqua. Scripts, such as Sylphide (p. 120) and Zirkularschrift Hortensia (p. 121), which were decidedly easier to read and more elegant, were used for a variety of social documents. Volumes of specimen books produced for printers and compositors were devoted to *Werbeschrift* (advertising type), and this added to the large amounts of Antiqua that had reached critical mass, as well as novelty scripts, such as Flotte Werbeschrift (pp. 126–27), which itself came in both very fluid and rigid styles.

German lettering and typefaces were characterized (if not also hampered) by an abundance of accents, yet in the design of the more novel scripts accent marks were conveniently eliminated: either for reasons of aesthetics or rebellion, accents and ligatures were seen as hindering legibility. Even as movements for the standardized beautification of difficult-to-read script writing grew in Germany, not every designer agreed to follow rigid typographic dicta. The regime, they believed, should not dictate design details, where, according to Mies van der Rohe, God resided.

Unlike the other countries represented in this book, German cursives were not slavishly beholden either to curvilinear Jugendstil (Art Nouveau) or rectilinear Art Deco. Although some German advertising and packaging graphics were designed in the French or British manner, which echoed the Italian and American styles, decorative scripts were not as prevalent. Heavy brush scripts (like the poster for *Die Raumkunst*, p. 136) were dominant. Precision, too, was the hallmark of German scripts, even those with an ad hoc appearance.

A huge number of variegated and stylized Fraktur faces filled the foundry specimen books. They were designed in all the Black Letter forms and included: Textualis, the most calligraphic form; Schwabacher, the most widely used Black Letter in Germany; Cursiva, a simplified form of Textualis; and Rotunda, an Italian Black Letter. But the Germans were nothing if not masters of expressive graphic design, from type to logos. So not only were many of the Fraktur faces uniquely beautiful and starkly bold, but the non-*volk* scripts, some even influenced by Venetian scripts, also exuded a distinct Germanic flair. ❧

Mod
Sch
Sche
' in

erne

ften

olz

A B C D E F G G H
I J K L M N O P Q
R S S T U V W W

1 2 3 4 5 · X Y Z · 6 7 8 9 0

a b b c d d e f f g h h i j k l l m n o p q r r

Cyclamen · s s t u v w x y z · Original

‹VENETIANISCHE SCHREIBSCHRIFT› · SCHRIFTGIESSEREI GENZSCH & HEYSE, HAMBURG.

A B C D E F G H I J K L
M N O P Q R S T U V W

a b b c d d e f g · X Y Z · h h i j k l m n o p

1 2 3 4 5 · q r s t u v w x y z z · 6 7 8 9 0

Venezuela · Requiem · Testament

rait

logue

02

N·MIFFLIN
CO.
NEW YORK

*Jap Rose
Soap.*

*James S. Kirk & Co
Chicago*

oß

aria

otti

*Ludwig
Thoma
Die
Medaille*

MARCEL
Flirt
PRÉVOST

Parfumerie

GER & GALLET

Paris

*The
House
of the
Seven
Gables
by
Nathaniel
Hawthorne*

ABCDEFGHIJKLM

NOPQRSTUVWXYZ

AAAELLK · bdaaRLEM

abcdefghijklmnopqrstuvwxyz

12345 · Philadelphia · 67890

Fahrenheit · Glasgow · Lieutenant

«SYLPHIDE» · ORIGINALERZEUGNIS DES HAUSES J. G. SCHELTER & GIESECKE, LEIPZIG.

ABCDEFGHIJKL

MNOPQRSTUVW

1 2 3 4 5 · p q r s t u v w y z

Anecdote · Rothschild · Potsdam

ZIRKULARSCHRIFT HORTENSIA · SCHRIFTGIESSEREI EMIL GURSCH, BERLIN.

DUMONT · LORD · BUDGET

Mandoline

Confession · Rousseau

ABCDEFGHIJKLMNOPQ

12345 · RSTUVWXYZ · 67890

abcdefghijklmnopqrstuvwxyz

A B C
D E F G
N O P Q
V W X Y
h i j k l m n o p q r
1 2 3 4 5 6 7 8 9 0

Völker

Mit Ato- oder Bandzugfeder zu schreiben.

KLM

STU

Z abcdefg

wxyzZ

Karste

123

A B C C

F K L V

R S T U

Z a b c d e f g h

w x y z z ſt ſz

$\mathcal{F}\ \mathcal{G}\ \mathcal{H}$

$\mathcal{O}\ \mathcal{P}\ \mathcal{Q}$

$\mathcal{W}\ \mathcal{X}\ \mathcal{Y}$

$n\ o\ p\ q\ w\ \int s\ t\ u\ v$

$3\ 4\ 5\ 6\ 7\ 8\ 9\ 0$

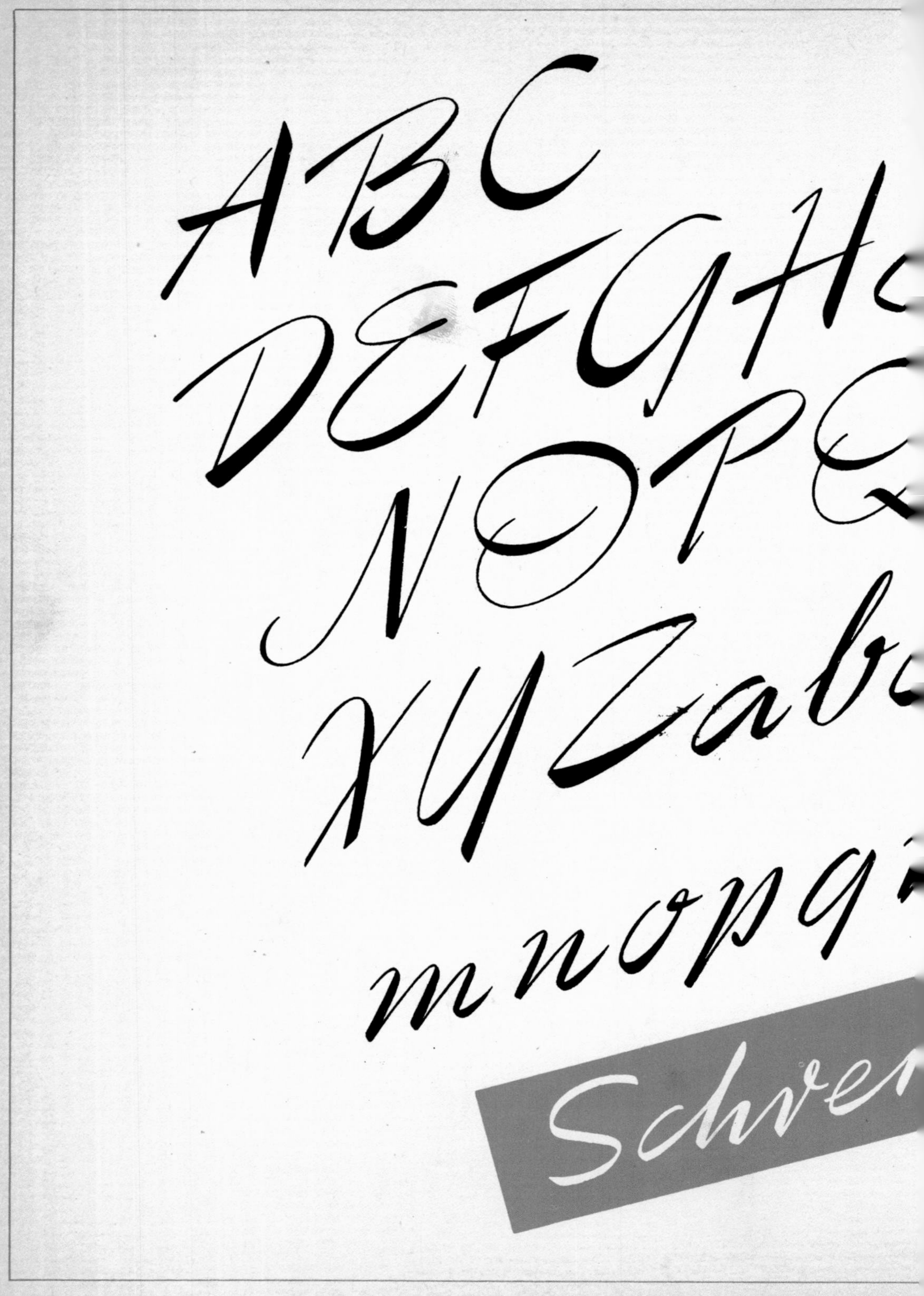

ABC
DEFGHs
NOPQ
XYZaba
mnopqi
Schrei

m

TUVW

ghijkl

wxyz3

ift

123456789

Mit einem
Spitzpinsel zu schreiben.

$$A B C D E F$$

$$N O P R S T$$

$$a b c d e f g h i j k l m$$

Diese Schrift v

geschrieben.

flott mager G e

13720 20 Punkte ca. 8,50 kg 18 A 64 a   *Die Entwic*

13724 24 Punkte ca. 9,50 kg 16 A 56 a   *Heilquellen*

13728 28 Punkte ca. 11 kg 14 A 50 a   *Konzert a*

13736 36 Punkte ca. 12 kg 10 A 36 a   *Wissens*

13748 48 Punkte ca. 13,50 kg 6 A 20 a   *Rund*

tzes Original-Erzeugnis

chitektur bis zur Gegenwart

e im Rhein-Maingebiet

ner Philharmoniker

Natur und Kunst

-Ausstellung

Die deutsche Meist

Schalke 04 und VfB Stuttgart bestreiten das Endspiel um

Das mit Spannung erwartete Treffen in Düsseldorf zwischen Schalke 04 und Polizei Chemnitz endete vor 45000 Zuschauern mit einem 3:2 (3:1)-Siege des Titelverteidigers. Eine Überraschung gab es beim Vorschlußrundenkampf in Leipzig. Hier schlug der VfB Stuttgart, obwohl er in der zweiten Halbzeit nur mit 10 Mann spielte, den VfL Benrath mit 4:2 (2:1) Treffern. Bei Benrath fehlte der bekannte Internationale Hohmann. Der Sieg der Stuttgarter war auf Grund ihres nie erlahmenden Eifers verdient.

VfL Benrath - VfB Stuttgart 2:4 (1:2)

Leipzig, 2. Juni. Das Vorschlußrundenspiel des VfL Benrath mit dem württembergischen Meister, VfB Stuttgart, wurde auf dem Leipziger VfB-Platz vor über 20000 Zuschauern ausgetragen und endete mit dem überraschenden Siege der Stuttgarter. Die Württemberger kämpften ähnlich wie vor kurzem gegen die SpVgg. Fürth mit einem nie erlahmenden Eifer. Sie hatten das Pech, fast die ganze zweite Spielhälfte mit nur

teidigung oft i
der Pause sch
nerische Tor.
abwehren, ak
Linksaußen I
Nach dem S
plötzlich aus
erhöhte sie
sich durchg
wurde Wei
Seine zehn
sprung, ke
einen Ha
gebnis au
doch nicl
Tor ihren
bei dene

Scha

Im Dü
schluß

Steilvorlage von Munkelt auf und schoß an dem herauslaufe
den Mellage vorbei ein (1:1). Für wenige Minuten war Schal
etwas überrascht, fand sich aber sofort wieder und lieferte da
bis zur Pause ein fast fehlerfreies Spiel. Nach verschiede
Eckbällen kamen die Westfalen in der 26. Minute wiede
zum Führungstreffer. Pörtgen hatte Kuzzorra in Schußstell
gebracht, der Halblinke stand frei und schoß ruhig und ü
legt ein. Der deutsche Meister blieb weiterhin überlege
kam auch zehn Minuten vor der Pause zum dritten Tor. Ca
setzte den Linksaußen Urban gut ein, die Flanke gelan
Kalvitzki, der den Vorsprung auf 3:1 erhöhte.
Nach der Pause wurde Chemnitz überraschender Weise
überlegen. Die Gäste verstärkten ihren Sturm und b
jetzt einen ebenbürtigen Partner, zumal Schalke das Inn
übertrieb. Nur für 10 Minuten waren die Westfalen He
Lage, dann kamen sie vor allem nach dem zweiten Geg
mitunter in Bedrängnis. In der 23. Minute konnte Me
Ball nicht festhalten, Helmchen stürmte heran, scho
Schweinfurt lenkte den Ball über die Latte. Den Elf
stoß verwandelte Helmchen sicher. Schalke ist jet
Dingen darauf bedacht, den Vorsprung zu halter
auch bei beiderseits äußerst kritischen Situatione

st?

ft in Köln

uten vor Beginn
arf auf das geg-
e den Ball zwar
heranbrausenden

t des VfB Stuttgart
nach zwei Minuten
alblinke Bökle hatte
chossen. Bald darauf
n Rest des Spiels aus.
ner Energie den Vor-
ern, daß Rasselnberg
lte und damit das Er-
mberger ließen sich je-
ießlich durch ein viertes
ährend die Rheinländer,
n fehlte, sehr nachließen.

lizei Chemnitz 3:2

en am Sonntag zu dem Vor-
sche Fußball-Meisterschaft
chalke 04 und dem Sachsen-
niger als 45000 Interessenten,
Umgebung von Gelsen-
Hans

v. Cramm in Paris gesc

Bei schwülem Wetter und bei bedecktem Himm
Sonntag in Paris die Endspiele um die französ
meisterschaften ausgetragen. Die erste Entsch
Fraueneinzel zwischen Frau Krahwinkel-Spe
Mathieu. Die Deutschdänin spielte mit eiserne
klug und überwand die französische Rivalin
leicht mit 6:2, 6:1. Bis zum dritten Spiel ga
Geplänkel, bei 2:1 griff aber die frühere Esse
nur noch ein Spiel ab. Ebenso ging es im zw

Perry gegen v. Cramm 6:3, 3

Sofort nach Beendigung des Treffens Krahw
athieu wurde mit der Entscheidun
begonnen. D

Wohnu

Das · Bürg

Verein

Münchner · Y

Die ·

Kl

· Die

Jah

1912·

Er

Kunst

ge·heim·

t·der

natsschrift

m:

t

16
17

135

Wohnungskun[st]

DAS·BÜRGERLÍCHE·HEI
VEREINIGT·MIT·DER·MÜNC
NER·HALBMONATSSCHRI

Die·Raumkuns[t]

HANSMANN

Gebrauchsgraphik

6

ATIONAL ADVERTISING ART $\frac{6}{1950}$

ABCD
IKLM
RSTU
abcdef
mnopq
12345 y

138

F GH
OPQ
exy
ghikl
tuvnx
67890

Otto Heim, Niedersedlitz-Dresden

139

A B C D E

L M N O

U V V

a b c d e f g

q r s t

1 2 3 4 5

Gesetzlich geschützt.

G H I J K

L M R S T

U V Y Z Z

k l m n o p

W X X Y Z Z

7 8 9 0

Otto Heim, Niedersedlitz-Dresden

ABCD
KLM
STUV
abcdefg
opqrstu
123

GHI
DQR
XYZ
klmn
vxyz
67890

Otto Heim, Niedersedlitz-Dresden

Illustrierter
Film-Kurier

So gefällst Du mir

116–17. Specimen sheet showing Black Letter ornamented with Art Deco tropes for Moderne Schriften from the Berthold Foundry, Berlin, *c*. 1928.

118–19. Specimen pages of Venetianische Schreibschrift from the catalog of Genzch & Heyse, Hamburg, 1929.

120–21. Specimen page of Sylphide (left) and Zirkularschrift Hortensia (right) from the catalog of J. G. Schelter & Giescke, Leipzig, 1929.

122–23. Specimen page of Schöne Schreibschrift from an advertising typeface portfolio, *c*. 1935.

124–25. Specimen page of Flüssiger Werbezug from an advertising typeface portfolio, *c*. 1935.

126–27. Specimen page of Flotte Werbeschrift from an advertising typeface portfolio, *c*. 1935.

128–29. Specimen page of Schönschreibschrift from an advertising typeface portfolio, *c*. 1935.

130–31. Specimen page of Flott from a type catalog, printer and date unknown.

132–33. Example of script typeface used in a sports newspaper, 1935.

134–35. Hand-drawn Black Letter for the masthead of an art magazine, 1912.

136. Hand-drawn Black Letter for the cover of *Die Raumkunst* magazine, 1913.

137. Masthead for *Gebrauchsgraphik*, a design magazine, employing script and Roman letters, 1950.

138–43. Specimen sheets by Otto Heim from a portfolio of letterforms for sign painters, *c*. 1910.

144. Customized handwriting 'So gefällst du mir,' on the cover of *Illustrierter Film-Kurier*, 1935.

Italian

EVERY NATION PRODUCES FAMILIES OF SCRIPTS UNIQUE TO THEIR NATIVE CULTURES. YET OF ALL THE WORLD'S scripts, Italian faces from the 1920s through the 1950s were arguably more distinctive—and obviously more joyfully Italian—than any others. The reason for this distinction might well be traced back to the Italian lettering tradition: Italy was, of course, the birthplace of Latin letters. But the introduction of novel cursive alphabets, particularly the stylized Art Moderne (or Art Deco) families, may have been a critical response to the classical legacy. "Enough of this classicism," a type designer might say, "let's party!" Which is an apt way to categorize the more festive Italian scripts.

The styles that truly jump off the Italian type-book pages are those that take liberties with conventional form. Apart from the vintage calligraphic scripts commonly used on late 19th-century billheads (like those shown for Napoleone Bianchi and Luigi Ajello, pp. 150–51), which mimicked pristine business and social handwriting—and were readily available to printing shops through the leading type foundries—the most exceptional commercial scripts were loaded with quirks. And while not always well composed according to accepted typographic standards, they nonetheless benefited from eccentricities born of the human hand.

The logo for *Le Grandi Firme* (p. 171) is what might best be called "script brute," a common Italian script and a rather heavy-handed rendering that suggests early graffiti. Conversely, the rather brutish masthead for *La Donna Fascista* (p. 172), a women's periodical of the Mussolini era, presents the allure of fashion—womanly yet not too feminine. The scripts of the Fascist period were actually more angular and hard-edged, in keeping perhaps with the ideological belief that women were not to be overly sensual. This was arguably reflected in type.

How the words of a particular language look when set in type also determines how striking a typeface will be. Scripts, which are typographic "voices," are the perfect complement for the Italian tongue. The script announcing "Spremuta naturale di puro zucchero..." (p. 201) reads as though it springs forth from beautiful pursed lips, and when it comes to vino the names Montresor, Moscato, and Lambrusco flow off the labels like the reds and whites out of the bottles (pp. 202–3). Similarly, one can virtually see the Italian vocal gestures in the bold-typeset words, "di Limone," "di Fragola," "di Lampone" and "di Amarena" on the labels for Zuegg flavored syrups (pp. 204–5).

Scripts are best appreciated—and best "heard"—when they are viewed in context. The words "Fiorisa" and "Vaniglia" whisper off the Art Deco packages for facial powder (p. 207). Even the scripts in school textbooks rhythmically parse the words into a kind of curvilinear poetics. Learning to write script Ls and Ps as shown on the *quaderno* (notebook) pages (pp. 210–11) had to be a pleasurable task for the children who choreographed words on paper as though they were letter ballets.

The most glorious of all Italian scripts were the signs made from iron, glass, and neon for all kinds of eateries, bars, hotels, and retail stores. Curvaceous handwriting is at its most eloquent—and at times elegant— in the one-word titles for restaurants like Tagliavini and Trattoria Otello (pp. 216, 218). Common words, like *barbiere* (barber) and *calzature* (footwear) take on new importance when scripted in neon and metal (pp. 220–21). Some signs are little more than three-dimensional versions of the two-dimensional printed piece. Mosaic scripts that feature on signs in Venice are actually set into the street (p. 222). They may have inherent inconsistencies, but are nonetheless beautiful.

Although Italian designers favored and reprised certain script styles—like the bold outline scripts for Impermeabili Ettore Moretti (an umbrella company, pp. 226–27) and Bimbi d'Italia (baby food, pp. 228–29)—during the 1920s through the 1950s the range of uniquely Italian scripts was huge. Most of them were customized by hand. And while some were based on more formal typefaces, the majority of them were born of the imagination. Some echoed handwriting mannerisms, while others derived from unconventional sources. The Futurists used sharp-edged, speed-infused gothic typefaces, but nonetheless influenced the design of many scripts that, rather than having a bourgeois appearance and significance (anathema to the radical Futurists), looked as though they were created either in or by a machine. Such were the varieties that defined Italian scripts. 🙢

ROBES
Confections
Modes

Duplicata

A. Gnardi

Madame la Marquise Bi

Piazza Ca

Duplicata

vier 1893

née subira un in

Piazza Castello, 26.

Napoleone Bia

Torino, li

DARE Sig.

Torino, il 4 Dicembre 1884

ASPORTI
nze. 7.

Luigi Ajello

Sig.r M.se Alessandro Guasco di Bisio

Bukarest

Lit. B. Marchisio

SCIALLI
FOULARDS PERCALLI
ed Articoli per Lutto
FLANELLE
DRAPPERIE, LANERIE
PLAIDS
COPERTE DA VIAGGIO
SARTORIA
PER

MAGAZZINO DI

Antonio
successore QUIRICO E
TORINO
Via Roma angolo Via Cavour · Piazza Capr

Sig.ª Marchesa Risio - Gattinara

chi

9 C 18

Gattinara

Torino, il 24/4

Gio. Cappa e Fig

VIA ROMA N.º 10 (CASA VITALE

Calzoleria
di
Agostino Bera
Via Fontanella di Borghese 59.ª
Roma

E. Il Sig. M. Guasco di Bisio

Gioielliere

→ E ←

FABBRICANTE OREFICE

TORINO

Mich...

Sig. Marchese

per i seguenti oggetti pagabili in Torino

1889		
Xbre 18	Un braccia...	
	g. 127½. con...	
	oro g. 12,30 co...	

152

Gennaio 1893

ele Franco

Via Alfieri, 4.

Bisio .... Dare

contanti senza sconto

Garzini, Wolf & C.

le tto con bill
off. 9. 4 3/8.
asticcio 900

ROBES Confections Modes

J. A. Amonton

Madame la Marquise Bizzozer

Via Carignano, 5

Toute facture non payée dans le délai d'une année subira un intérêt de 5%.

TORINO, le 24 Septembre 1898

1898			
	1 Jaquette drap mousse		90
	1 Robe beige brodée		75
	1 Robe bleu Mlle Schuster		100
	1 Robe étamine laine		15
	Manches dentelle pour un corsage satin		
	Parfait une robe rouge façon corsage		180
24	cape chinée garni dentelle		

Description		Importo
Façon d'une robe rose garnie nœuds	"	=
Louis XV paillette argent. Corsage garni velours.	"	180
mousse. et dentelle guipure écru	"	76
Façon 3.10 ottoman	"	20
Ceinture de la robe	"	=
1 Robe moire jaune garnie sa dentelle	"	285
et ceinture moire noire	"	=
Façon d'une robe vert nil fourni taffetas	"	175
pour corsage, doublure de jupe et ruban	"	20
Ceinture de la robe	"	=
Façon d'un grand vêtement satin et velours	"	100
brodé fourni doublure soie	"	175
1 Collet beige garni dentelle	"	Lire 19.11

Avvertasi in acconto e consegnato riceduto " 1.000

Restano Lire 911.

155

TESSITURA

DI

Coperte in Seta sistema Jacquard

COPERTE SCOZZESI & RIGATE

SETERIE

S. E. Sig.^{ra} Marchesa Teresa

per le seguenti merci speditevi co

CENTIMETRI	PEZZI	
90×150	5	copertine seta
180×220	1	coperta seta, g
		spesa postale
1900		

tono reclami nè ritorni.

Settembre 3 spedizione fattale

156

A. Bianchi

Bellagio, li 19 Agosto 190

Bisio — Novi — Dare

pacco le pagamento per cassa

Tip. Lit. R. Longatti - Como

		£ 3 = £	15 =
...allo e bianco		7 =	7 =
...ud ...			1 =
		£	93 =

A. Bianchi

Fornitori di S. A. R. il Duca d'Aosta

PRIMI APPLICATORI

DELLA

Lavatura a Evaporazione

per sete e velluti

SPECIALITÀ

LAVAGGIO STOFFE BIANCHE

Tintura Stoffe

e Maglie Cotone

V.va

Vi

Signora

le seguenti pagabili in

2 ƒ guanti e

TINTORIA

Fondata nel 1848

Nicol & Figli

Mazzini (già Borgonuovo) 4

Torino, 10 — 2   1895

Marchesa Bisio

2 Corso V. E.   **DARE**

ino

Telo rosa giallo la 2

Pagato subito

Orticoltore e Fiorista

Tommaso Baracchi

Contrada Sgarzeria, 12 - MODENA - Contrada Sgarzeria, 12

€ 2,00

eguisce
unque in fiori
CIALITÀ
MORTUARIE
DITA
PIANTE

li _____ 191 5

Dare

Per una corona con fiori freschi
con nastro 35

Saldato li 3...
Baracchi Tommaso

MARCA DA BOLLO — CENT. DIECI

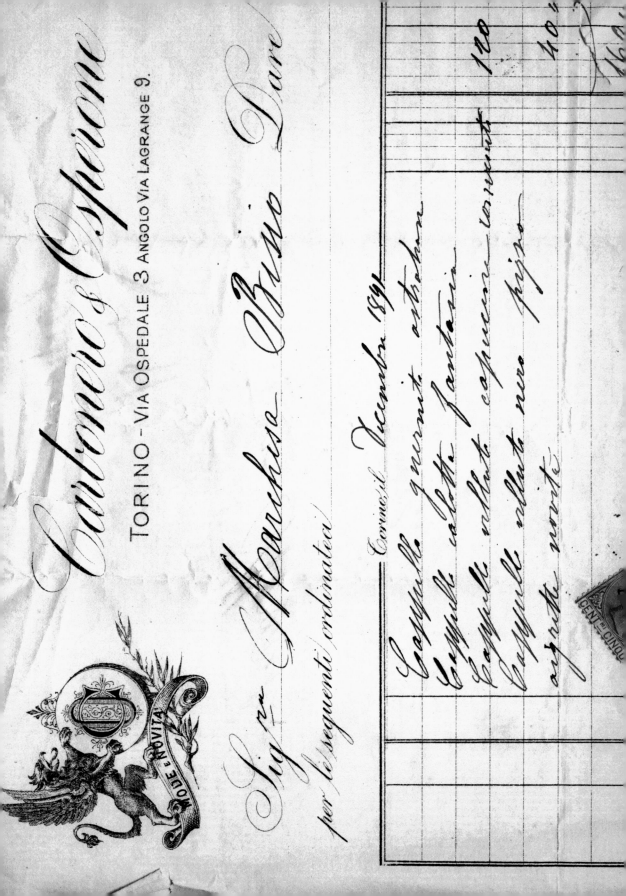

Cartonero & Spriani

TORINO – VIA OSPEDALE 3 ANGOLO VIA LAGRANGE 9.

MODE E NOVITA

Sig.ra Marchesa Bisso Dare

per li seguenti ordinateci

Torino, il ... Dicembre 1891

		120
Cappello guarnito astrakan		
Cappello cotto fantasia		
Cappello velato cappuccio ...		
Cappello velato nero figno		40
aigrette nere		

CENT 50 CINQUE

SPECIALITÀ IN CORREDI BIANCHERIA

ANGOLO
VIE GARIBALDI
E VENTI SETTEMBRE

F.co C.

PROVVEDITORE

Illma Sig.ra M.sa

le seguenti vendute d'accordo

TORINO, 5

40 5 Cm Nansouk

LIVERO e C.

DI S.A.R. IL DUCA D'AOSTA E REAL FAMIGLIA

...iò Gattinara Dare

...pronti contanti senza sconto.

...uglio 1888

Lire F.º Doyen.

... " 80

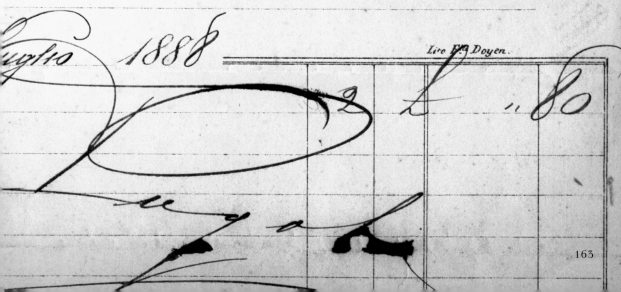

163

Vetreria D...

Negozio: PIAZZALE S. EUFEMIA, 48 - TEL. 34-64

Lavorazione del vetro e magazzeno:
VIA CARLO SIGONIO, 17 - TELEFONO 2800

Sig Barbieri

Fattura N. 292

Per le seguenti merci speditevi a mezzo

Pagamento al mio domicilio

La merce viaggia a rischio e pericolo del Committente anche se venduta franco destino. - Non si
rifiuta al suo arrivo. - Prima di ritirare i colli verificare la confezione ed il peso declinando og...

m. 10 oh *canetta d...*

Stucco du vetr...

nte **_Malagoli_**

MODENA, 6 - 11 - 44

/H. Prof. Armando

Modena

vi sottopongo fattura di L. 117, 80

Vetro a	10	£	100.00
		"	15.00
		£	115.00
		"	2.30
Sup. Entrata		£	117.30
Totale		£	

Vittorio Emanuele III

PER GRAZIA DI DIO E PER VOLONTÀ DELLA NAZIONE

58

Re d'Italia

Sulla proposta del Presidente del Consiglio dei Ministri, Nostro Ministro ad interim per gli Affari della Guerra.

Abbiamo decretato e decretiamo:

Articolo Unico

Nel precedente decreto relativo al sottonominato ufficiale di complemento del Corpo d'Amminist.ne sono autorizzate le rettifiche sottoindicate:

Grado	Cognome e Nome		Rettificazione autorizzata	
Tenente R.D. 11-1-1925	Sala	Giovanni di Antonino	Sala	Giovanni Battista di Antonino
Sottotenente R.D. 19-7-1923	Ambrogio	Sante di Giuseppe	Ambrogio	Santo di Giuseppe

Il predetto Nostro Ministro è incaricato dell'esecuzione del presente Decreto che sarà registrato alla Corte dei Conti

Dato a Roma addì 15 novembre 1925.

Reg.to alla Corte dei Conti

166

Emanuele

Beatrice Roma

Antonio Emilia

Cic. 8 - Classe B-f

Piermarini

Cic. 10 - Classe B-l

Dantesco

Manlio

Cic. 18 - Classe C-o — Cic. 20 - Classe D-b
Cic. 25 - Classe D-p — Cic. 30 - Classe E-m

Londra

Nel prezzo vi sono compresi i finali e la spaziatura in proporzione della polizza ordinata

Dans le prix des lettres sont compris les finals et les espaces en proportion de la police comandée

Cic. 15 - Classe C-g

Roma

Anno I. N° 1   Milano Ottobre 1926.   C. C. Posta

Excelsior

EDIZIONI
VITAGLIANO
MILANO
L. 5.

GLORIOSA
CASA EDIT.
ITALIANA
MILANO

COLLEZIONE DEL CERCHIO BLU - n. 36

Per essere bella

reportage di
Louis Léon-Martin

1.50

Le grandi firme ed.
TORINO

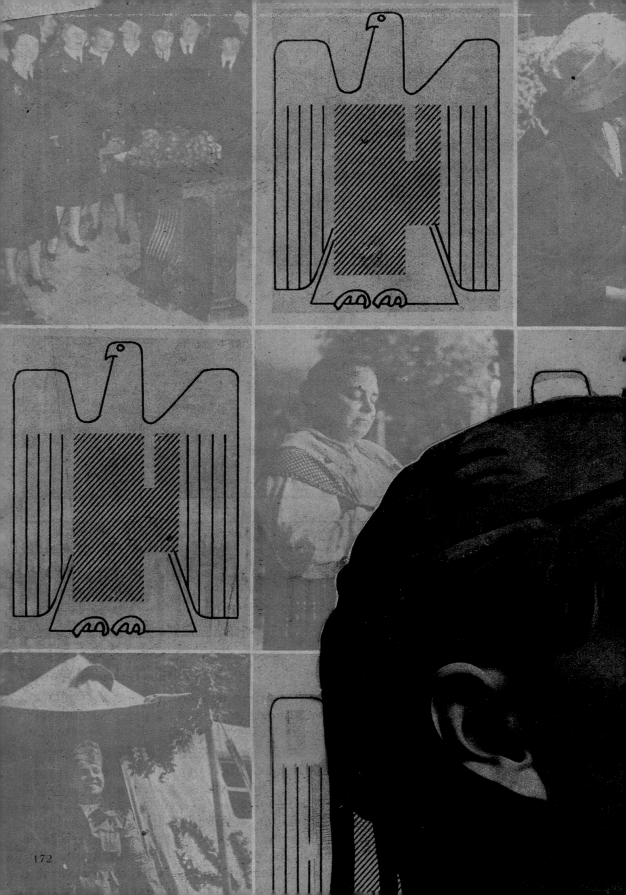

la donna fascista

raion

fiocco

Italviscosa

SNIA · CISA · CHATILLON

Rem

INDUSTRIA ABBIGLIAMENTO MASCHILE

CARATE BRIANZA

Una sorgente di profumato ottimismo

Poche gocce di Acqua di Coty, una leggera frizione ed ecco che una nuova energia penetra in voi. L'effetto è sorprendente. Un'ondata di freschezza profumata circola nel vostro organismo; una sensazione di sereno benessere vi ridona forza e vitalità.

Più pura, fresca e leggera di ogni altra l'Acqua di Coty è la sintesi perfetta di tutti i fragranti effluvi della primavera: infatti essa contiene l'essenza stessa dei fiori e delle frutta più scelte. Se invece preferite un'Acqua di Colonia più aromatica e profumata, domandate l'Acqua di Colonia Coty, Capsula Rossa, che, pur serbando i pregi della prima, unisce il vantaggio di profumare più intensamente e più a lungo.

ACQUA DI

COTY

Capsula Verde

ANNO X - N. 178   Lire **1,50**   15 GENNAIO 1934-XII

CONTO CORRENTE POSTALE

il dramma

quindicinale di commedie di
grande successo, diretto da
LUCIO RIDENTI

Ettore Petrolini in Egitto

EDITRICE "LE GRANDI FIRME" - TORINO

15 GIUGNO 1934-XII

ANNO XI - TORINO - CONTO-CORRENTE POSTALE

le grandi firme

quindicinale di novelle

ei massimi scrittori, diretto d

Pitigrilli:

UIGI ANTONELLI
Il Saltimpalo

ARLO VENEZIANI
Chiudiamo la valigia

ALENTIN WILLIAMS
L'ultima scena del film

C. PHILIPS
L'onore

APPER
Una donna adorabile

ALBERTO DONAUD
La riffa

VITTORIO GUERRIER
Lucienne Boyer

H. DE VERE STACPOO
Malia dell'Est

RENÉ JEANN
Potenza delle lacrime

J. BEESTO
Lo spirito della notte

UMERO 240

LIR 1,50

Leonardo Merrick: Il cacciatore
di fantasmi, CLAN

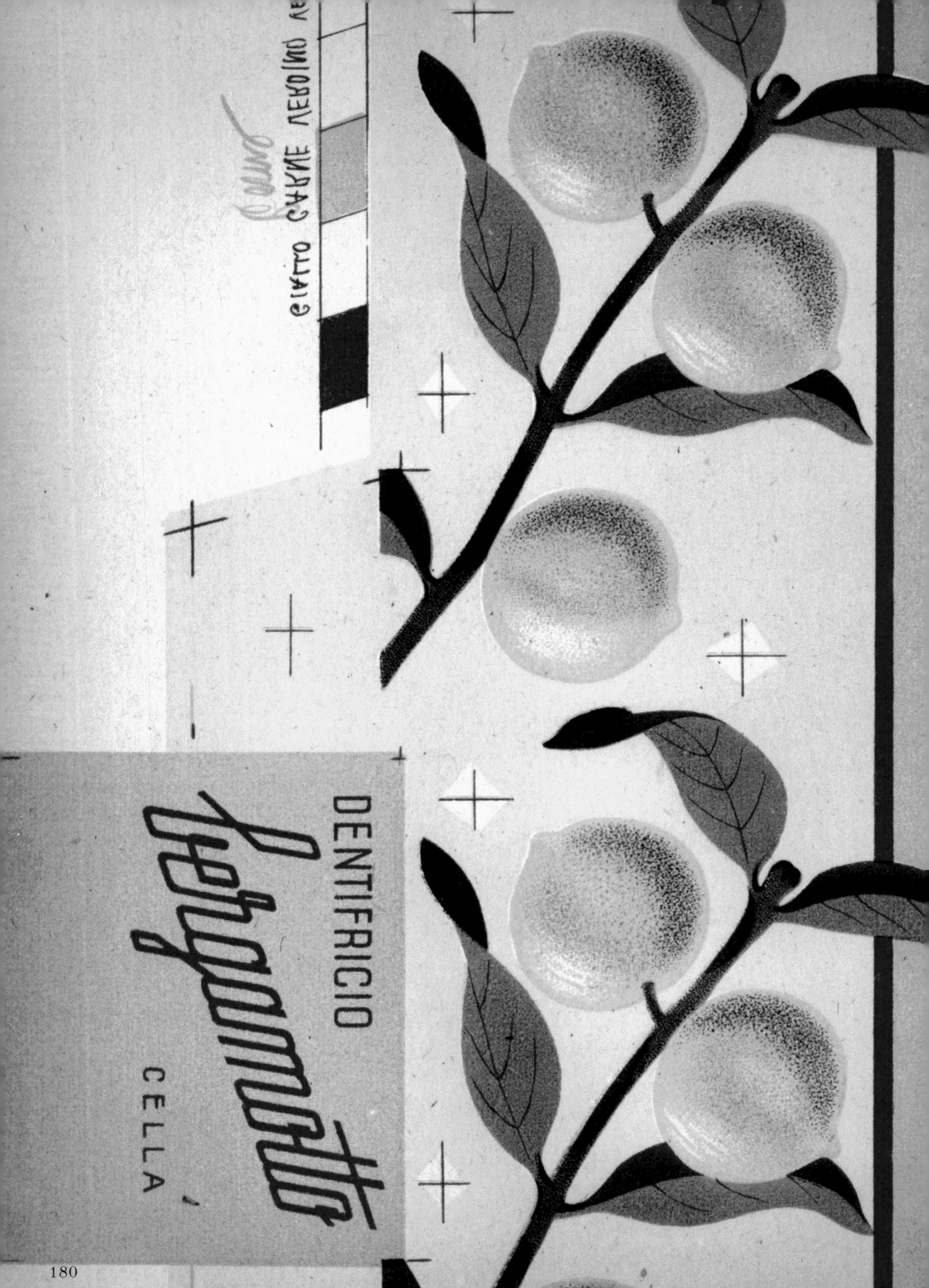
DENTIFRICIO
Bergamotto
CELLA
GIALLO CARNE VERDINO VA

DENTIFRICIO

bergamotto

CELLA

Il dentifricio BERGAMOTTO è una specialità preparata secondo una nuova formula creata da noti specialisti. I principii attivi dell'essenza di BERGAMOTTO ne determinano l'alto potere antisettico. Mantiene sana la bocca, rinnovando con l'uso costante il candore dello smalto. - Particolarmente consigliato ai fumatori.

CELLA - MILANO

DENTIFRICIO

bergamotto

CELLA

Il dentifricio BERGAMOTTO è una specialità preparata

Mélodies

de F. Paolo Tosti

Editions Ricordi

(PRINTED IN ITALY)   (IMPRIMÉ EN ITALIE)

Campionario
Caratteri e Fregi
Tipografici

Parti Prima
seconda e
Terza

Società Anonima

Ditta Nebiolo & Comp.
Torino

il Secolo Illustrato

ANNO VI - N. 5
1° Marzo 1918
SOCIETÀ EDITO-
RIALE ITALIANA

L. 1.—
Conto corrente colla Posta

"SOTTOSCRIZIONE,, | 1866 - Per la Santa Carabina | PAROLA GARIBALDINA.
| 1918 - Per la Liberazione e la Vittoria |

fino al 10 marzo 1918 rimane aperta la sottoscrizione pubblica al

PRESTITO CONSOLIDATO 5% NETT

lo Sport Illustrato

e la guerra

SOCIETÀ ANONIMA
PER COSTRVZIONI
AERONAVTICHE
ING. O. POMILIO & C.
SEDE·TORINO·CORSO FRANCIA 366
VFFICI·MILANO·ROMA·GENOVA

ANNO IV · N. 17
1 Settembre 1916
Edizione della
GAZZETTA
DELLO SPORT
Italia .. cent. 50
Estero .. ,, 75
Conto corrente colla Posta

Una nenia.

Ninna nanna,

Ninna nanna,

Ninna oooo.........

Ninna oooo.........

Amate il pane.

Rispettate il pane.

Onorate il pane.

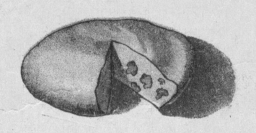

Buon Dio,
provvedi il pane per tutti!

La lucciola.

- Lucciola, lucciolina,
sei forse una stellina?
o sei una lampadina
pei bimbi di lassù?

Lucciola, lucciolina,
vieni un po' più vicina!
- Se volo più vicina
il lume non c'è più.

Lumaca, lumachina,
esci dalla casina !
Pioveva stamattina ;
bevi una gocciolina.
Lumaca, lumachina,
pesa la tua casina ?

Tacca Italiana   BASTARDA FILETTATA   *Classe* **D**

N. **2363 U.** - Corpo 36 (Rigenerare)   Kg. 5,85 (A-5, a-16)

Napoleone Bonaparte

13 Imperatore e Re 24

N. **2364 U.** - Corpo 48 (Rigettabile)   Kg. 7,35 (A-3, a-10)

Chambery Poitiers

Toulon Angoulême

N. **2365 U.** - Corpo 60 (Rigettare)   Kg. 9,25 (A-3, a-7)

Decoloramenti

N. **2366 U.** - Corpo 72 (Rigetto)   Kg. 11,50 (A-2, a-6)

Estremadura

Tacca Francese   SCRITTURA ITALICA   *Classe E*

N. **983** - Corpo 16 (Biacca)   Kg. 4,60 (A-10, a-90)

5 á conocer en el glorioso reinado de los Reyes Catolicos 3

N. **982** - Corpo 24 (Bezzo)   Kg. 5,65 (A-6, a-50)

Le grandi Scoperte del genio umano

Galileo Galilei = Marconi Guglielmo

N. **981** - Corpo 36 (Bertuccia)   Kg. 6,50 (A-4, a-24)

Monsieur Emile Langlois

Expositions des Parfuméries

N. **980** - Corpo 48 (Bertone)   Kg. 7,75 (A-2, a-12)

Officine Elettriche

Genovesi Ulderico

191

Tacca Francese   ## CARATTERI MANOSCRITTO   *Classe A*

N. 2107 - Corpo 12 (Mendace)   Kg. 3, – (A- 16, a-100)

Empezó el reinado de este trigésimo quinto y último rey godo, viviendo aún su antecesor Witiza, cuyos hijos había desterrado al Africa en mal hora, pues confabulándose con el conde Iulián

N. 2108 - Corpo 18 (Menide)   Kg. 4,50 (A- 16, a-80)

La Legislazione Norvegese stabilisce che ove un

23   *uomo ancora valido non trovi lavoro la*   45

Tacca Francese   ## CARATTERI A LAPIS   *Classe A*

N. 991 - Corpo 12 (Bidetto)   Kg. 2,50 (A- 10, a-60)

Nous avons l'honneur de porter à votre connaissance qu'à partir du Premier Septembre prochain, notre

N. 992 - Corpo 18 (Bietola)   Kg. 3,50 (A- 6, a-40)

Questa Serie di Caratteri a Lapis utile assai è ai Signori Tipografi, servendo

N. 993 - Corpo 24 (Bifolco)   Kg. 5,50 (A- 6, a-40)

Le donne saggie non hanno nè occhi nè orecchie e se ne vanno

Tacca Francese   SCRITTURA VERTICALE   *Classe* **D**

N. 2605 - Corpo 24 (Valere)   Kg. 4, – (A-4, a-40)

A B C D E F G H I J L M N O P Q R

Gli accenni a Kio, abitata dai Genovesi, al

Paradiso fatto dai Fiorentini in Rodi, alla

12 abcdefghijklmnopqrstuvxyzz 34

N. 2476 - Corpo 48 (Valeriana)   Kg. 6, – (A-2, a-12)

A B C D E F G H I L O

Cirene e l'Egeo, ricordi

di Fogazzaro il saluto

23 abcdehilmnorst 45

193

Tacca Francese   **SCRITTURA INGLESE**   *Classe E*

Il Maiuscolo serve tanto per l'occhio grande come per l'occhio piccolo.

N. **1431** - C. 16, occhio piccolo (Esculapio)   Kg. 4,50   N. **1426** - C. 16, occhio grande (Esarca)   Kg. 4,50

(A - 10, a - 90)   Solo minuscolo Kg. 3, –   (A - 10, a - 90)

Stanislao Cav. Romualdi   *Mario Fontanetta & C.°*

N. **1432** - C. 20, occhio piccolo (Escursione)   Kg. 6, –   N. **1427** - C. 20, occhio grande (Esattore)   Kg. 6, –

(A - 8, a - 80)   Solo minuscolo Kg. 4, –   (A - 8, a - 80)

Ministero Nazionale   *Inventor del Telefono*

N. **1433** - C. 24, occhio piccolo (Esedra)   Kg. 8, –   N. **1428** - C. 24, occhio grande (Eschio)   Kg. 8, –

(A - 8, a - 80)   Solo minuscolo Kg. 5, –   (A - 8, a - 80)

Aniceto Mariano   *Antonio Bobbio*

N. **1434** - C. 28, occhio piccolo (Esercente)   Kg. 9, –   N. **1429** - C. 28, occhio grande (Escogitare)   Kg. 9, –

(A - 6, a - 60)   Solo minuscolo Kg. 6, –   (A - 6, a - 60)

Edmondo Franco – *Rieti Novara*

N. **1430** - Corpo 42 (Escubile)   Kg. 8,50 (A - 4, a - 16)

Mademoiselle Renaudin

N. **1784** - Corpo 72 (Illudere)   Kg. 11, – (A - 2, a - 6)

Fratelli Davite

Tacca Francese | **SCRITTURA INGLESE NERETTA** | *Classe E*

N. **1774** - Corpo ▦ (Illabile)   Kg. 5,25
(A-10, a-90)

Sinfonia Pastorale

Concerto Accademico

N. **1548** - Corpo ²⁰▦ (Fortezza)   Kg. 6,50
(A-8, a-80)

Pharmacologique

N. **1549** - Corpo ²⁸▦ (Forziere)   Kg. 9,– (A-6, a-60)

Assedio di Troja

N. **1775** - Corpo 42 (Illegale)   Kg. 9,– (A-4, a-16)

Garibaldini

SCRITTURE INGLESI   *Classe E*

N. **3628 U.** - Corpo 60 (Rarità) *Tacca Italiana*   Kg. 8,25 (A-3, a-8)

Cimento Rustico

N. **1402** bis - Corpo 60 (Erario) *Tacca Francese*   Kg. 9,50 (A-2, a-6)

Ubaldo Farina

N. **1403** bis - Corpo ⁸⁴▦ (Erba) *Tacca Francese*   Kg. 15,– (A-2, a-6)

Emulazione

Tacca Francese   **SCRITTURA BASTARDA, CHIARA**   *Classe* **D**

N. 1129 C. 10 (Centesimi) Kg. 3, – (A - 12, a - 150)

Giovanni Battista Bodoni,
il grande intagliatore e incisore

N. 1130 C. 12 (Centrina) Kg. 3,75 (A - 12, a - 150)

Octubre Septiembre Agosto
Manuel Nicanor Anastasio

N. 1131 C. 16 (Centuria) Kg. 4,50 (A - 10, a - 90)

Esercitazioni Militari

N. 1132 - Corpo 20 (Ceppo) Kg. 5,75 (A - 8, a - 75)

Società Automobili Italia

N. 1133 - Corpo 28 (Cerbero) Kg. 5, – (A - 4, a - 40)

Collections Modernes

N. 1134 - Corpo 36 (Cerchione) Kg. 5, – (A - 2, a - 16)

Radiobalistiche

N. 1135 - Corpo 48 (Cerinta) Kg. 6,50 (A - 2, a - 12)

Industriale Fiorentino

Tacca Francese   **SCRITTURA BASTARDA, NERETTA**   *Classe* **D**

N. 1806 - Corpo 12 (Imbrattare) Kg. 4, – (A - 12, a - 150)

Florence, au Centre d'Italie, arrosée par l'Arno; superbes Mosaïque

N. 1807 - Corpo 16 (Imbrunare) Kg. 4, – (A - 8, a - 75)

Consiglio d'Amministrazione della Società Umanitaria

N. 1808 - Corpo 20 (Imbuto) Kg. 6, – (A - 8, a - 75)

Fundición Tipográfica y Talleres Mecánicos

N. 1809 - Corpo 28 (Imeneo) Kg. 5,50 (A - 4, a - 40)

Stabilimento Meccanico Nazionale

Tacca Italiana   **SCRITTURA AMERICANA**   *Classe E*

N. **1926 U.** - Corpo 12 (Rigoroso)   Kg. 1,70 (A-12, a-50)

Sucede muchas veces leemos en la Revista Cilena " Noticias Gráficas „ que 12 las Tintas deian traslucir el color del papel. Especialmente si el color 34

N. **1927 U.** - Corpo 16 (Rigovernare)   Kg. 2, – (A- 7, a-24)

Stagione lirica invernale al Teatro Dal Verme di Milano 78 Sonnambula - Cavalleria - Faust - Ballo Excelsior 93

N. **1928 U.** - Corpo 20 (Riguardare)   Kg. 2,60 (A- 7, a-24)

Manuale di Nomenclatura compilato dalla Professoressa Erminia Grondona-Lambertenghi

N. **1929 U.** - Corpo 24 (Riguardata)   Kg. 2,90 (A- 5, a-16)

La Storia del Risorgimento Nazionale Esposizione Internazionale di Belle Arti

N. **1930 U.** - Corpo 24 (Riguardevole)   Kg. 3, – (A- 4, a-15)

Un Premier Etude de Sculpture Ornementations et Décorations

Tacca Italiana | **SERIE GLORIA** | *Classe A*

N. **4801 U.** - Corpo 12 (Rimboscare)   Kg. 2,20 (A-14, a-72)

Non bisogna accontentarsi di lodare gli Uomini dabbene, ma bisogna imitarli 12345 L'animo fermo mostra che la Fortuna non ha potenza sopra di lui 67890

N. **4802 U.** - Corpo 16 (Rimbozzolire)   Kg. 2,75 (A-13, a-58)

Histoire complète des Beaux Arts et du Commerce en France 78 Nouvelles Marques de Fabriques - République de Pérou 45

N. **4803 U.** - Corpo 20 (Rimbrodolare)   Kg. 3, — (A-9, a-40)

Associazione Nazionale fra gli Impiegati Governativi Sede Centrale a Roma e Filiali a Milano, Torino

N. **4804 U.** - Corpo 28 (Rimbrodolone)   Kg. 3,85 (A-8, a-38)

Premiata Fabbrica Macchine Enologiche Stabilimento e Amministrazione in Roma

N. **4805 U.** - Corpo 36 (Rimbrottare)   Kg. 4,70 (A-5, a-16)

Comisión Directiva de la Escuela

N. **4806 U.** - Corpo 48 (Rimbrotto)   Kg. 6,25 (A-4, a-10)

Università di Bordeaux

Tacca Italiana   CORSIVI RÉCLAME   *Classe A*

N. 779 U. - Corpo 18 (Maliardo)   Kg. 3,15 (A-9, a-38)

Unione Nazionale delle Fonderie Caratteri
123 Torino Milano Bologna Palermo 456

N. 780 U. - Corpo 24 (Mallo)   Kg. 3,85 (A-7, a-24)

Établissement Mécanique Belge
78 Première Fabrique Armes 90

N. 928 U. - Corpo 36 (Frasca)   Kg. 4,75 (A-4, a-12)

Storia, Considerazione
Generale Riassuntiva

N. 929 U. - Corpo 42 (Fraschetto)   Kg. 5,50 (A-3, a-8)

Democratizzata

N. 930 U. - Corpo 60 (Freccia)   Kg. 9,25 (A-2, a-6)

Lombardia

Cooperativa Produ

SOCIETA' ANONIMA CAPITALE

SEDE

(Ascol

SUCC
GROTTAMMARE -
PORTO S.GIORGIO

MOSTRA DI ORTICOLTURA MAGGIO 1909
IN ASÇOLI PICENO
5 DIPLOMI DI PRIMO PREMIO CON MEDAGLIE

ESPOSIZIONE MILANO 1914
DIPLOMA DI GRAN PREMIO
CON GRANDE MEDAGLIA D'ORO DELLE LL.MM.D'ITALIA

FIERA CAMPIONARIA ASCOLI PICENO 1925
GRAN PRIX

MOSTRA AGRARIA ANCONA 1926
DIPLOMA DI GRAN PREMIO MEDAGLIA D'ORO

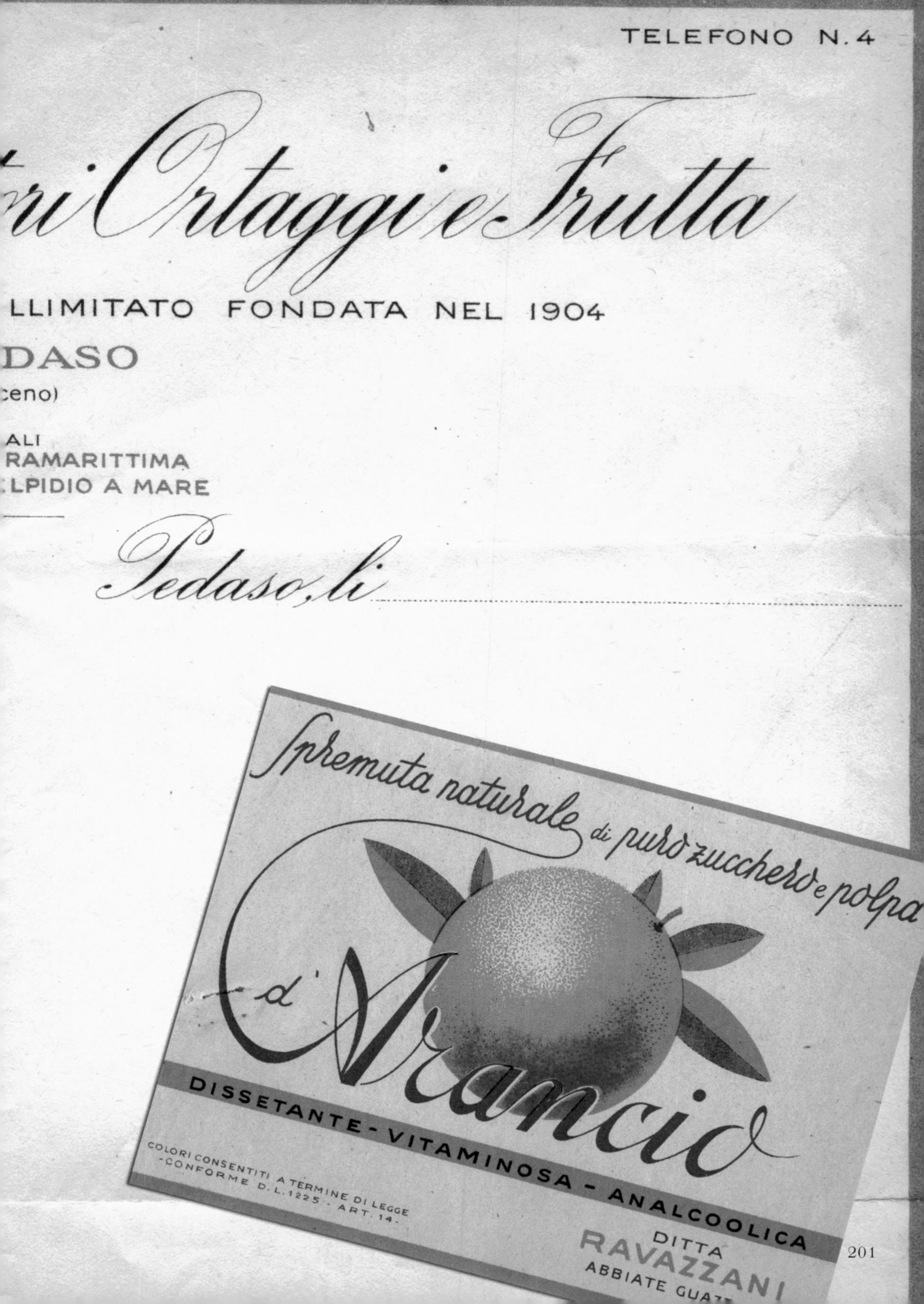

...ri Ortaggi e Frutta

LLIMITATO FONDATA NEL 1904

DASO

(ceno)

ALI

...RAMARITTIMA

...LPIDIO A MARE

Pedaso, li ....

Spremuta naturale di puro zucchero e polpa

d'Arancio

DISSETANTE - VITAMINOSA - ANALCOOLICA

COLORI CONSENTITI A TERMINE DI LEGGE
- CONFORME D.L. 1225 - ART. 14 -

DITTA

RAVAZZANI

ABBIATE GUAZ...

Lambrusco
DI SORBARA

CANTINA
BERTOLANI&F.
SCANDIANO

VINO PREGIATO

C.C.F. 1860

LAETIFICAT CORDA

Moscato
RISERVA

C. Chiarli & F.gli
Casa Fondata nel 1860

Italia

Modena

GARANTITO DI PURA FRUTTA CON 65% DI ZUCCHERO
CONFEZIONATO A NORMA R.D. 501 8/11/1923
Ravvivato con colore innocuo e consentito dalle prescrizioni di legge
Peso netto 1300 gr.
Sciroppo
di Limone
ZUEGG
LANA D'ADIGE
GARANTITO DI PURA FRUTTA CON 65% DI ZUCCHERO
CONFEZIONATO A NORMA R.D. 501 8/11/1923
Ravvivato con colore innocuo e consentito dalle prescrizioni di legge
Peso netto 1300 gr.
Sciroppo
di Fragola
naturale

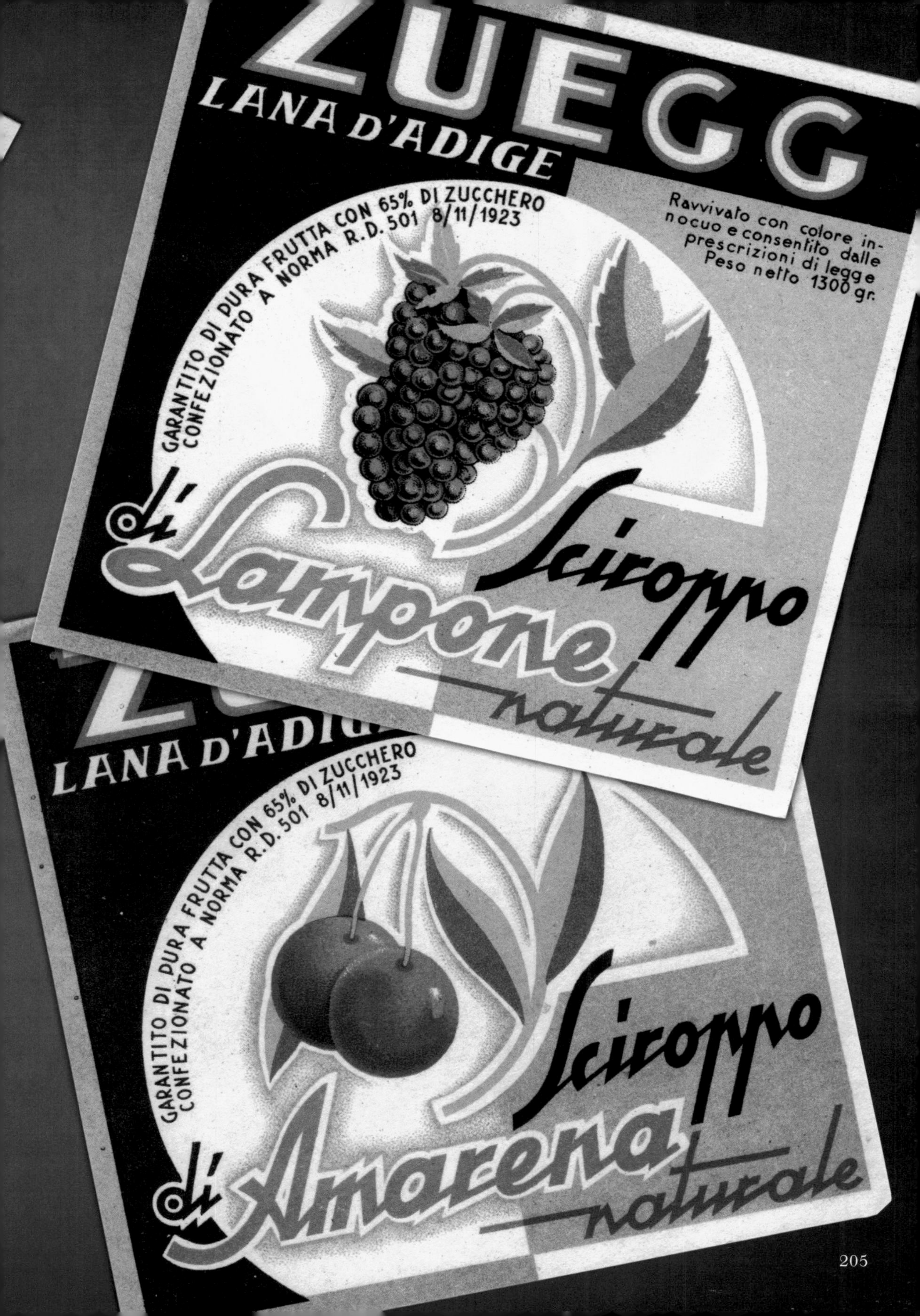

La Campana

Se tu metti attenzione
quando suona una campana,
no, non è un'illusione
e una voce quasi umana.
Lei ti sveglia al mattino
con il suo canto argentino,
suona poi a gran distesa
per i fedeli della chiesa.
Se c'è festa per bambini
i suoi suoni sembran strilli;
chiama assieme le sorele
sembran tante cascatele.
È gioiosa e clamorosa
se a l'altare c'è una sposa,
si fa in dieci si fa in venti
fa felici anche i parenti.
Suona triste e molto male
quando arriva un funerale,
a lei batte forte il cuore
e partecipa al dolore.
Ella batte a tutte l'ore
per il buon lavoratore,
se lo vede triste e stanco
il suo suono sembra pianto.
Da lontano il pescatore
fra i marosi sente il suono,
con l'orecchio l'accarezza
pensa questa è la salvezza.

lei t'invita alla preghiera
a tocchi lenti poi va via
mormorando Ave Maria.

Pasqua

Adesso che xe pasqua
no sta pensar a la fugassa,
quea magnandola
solo la te ingrassa.
Nutrissite de spirito
chel xe un forte siero,
che te farà star
sempre tanto esiero.
Perchè mia cara
che se ti xe ne
queo in fon
no te delude
Mi te go da u
se nol sarà a
magna la f
che te ingras
però cussi pesant
in paradiso no ti va.

Con questa ho vinto diploma e medaglia nel concor
da Napoli, studio Ungaretti; però bisognava scriver
in'Italiano, questo e il mio mestiere, e come lo ved
perche sono un po fantasiosa.

olte per strada guardando la moda di oggi mi
ene da pensare al setecento, c'è una diferenza grand
i lo scopo e quello di piacere a l'uomo.

Paragone

Mi so na dama del setecento
epoca d'oro e anca d'argento,
nei musei so più che amirada
e un pocheto forse imitada.
Ai nostri tempi bele o brute
portava tute bianche paruche,
adesso invesse i e ga piturae
bionde more rosse e sae.
El nostro viso bianco anca quelo
gaveva solo un picolo nelo,
adesso invesse e ga tuti i colori
come i quadri dei nostri pitori,
e se col caldo e va un poco a spasso
se missia i colori e deventa Picasso.
Nel nostro colo un veludin
co un camelo o un ritratin,
ancuo e porta igà un faroleto
che se ti e vardi e par un c
Si xe vero abastansa s
giera tute e nostre sp
ma adesso ghe manca
e te mostra tuta la pan
Cotole longhe e vaporose
giera l'orgoglio de tute e tos
e per passar co quel cotolon

208

la porta de casa la giera un porton.
Adesso e porte xe tute strete
  perchè ste tose xe tante bachete,
e porta e braghe cussì atilae
se vede solo gambe in'arcae,
una bluseta che par un veleto
e solo ghe manca el regipeto.
E nostre scarpe gaveva i fibioni
lore porta i zataroni
nee nostre man un picolo anelo
lore ghe na uno ogni delo.
Quando balavimo el minueto
se sventolavimo col ventaglieto,
  adesso co e bala e se remena
  par che e se grata tuta la schena.
Però no so qua per criticar
  el xe solo un modo de costatar,
  perchè la dona de tuti i tempi
  la se uguaglia nei sentimenti
E xe per questo che la va drio a la moda
se no mario no la ghe ne trova,
  La prepara l'esca la ghe zonta l'amo
per pescarse un bel Adamo.
  lu aboca povero fio,
  in silenzio el ghe va drio
  perche l'amo el ga ingiotio.

Giolo Elda

Una notte feci un sogno, mi pareva di volare
d'un tratto atterai, ma la fine no fu sodisfacen

S S S L L Li

Sara _ Lino

P P P P P Pie

*

* *

* * *

Piero Dante

*

* *

* * *

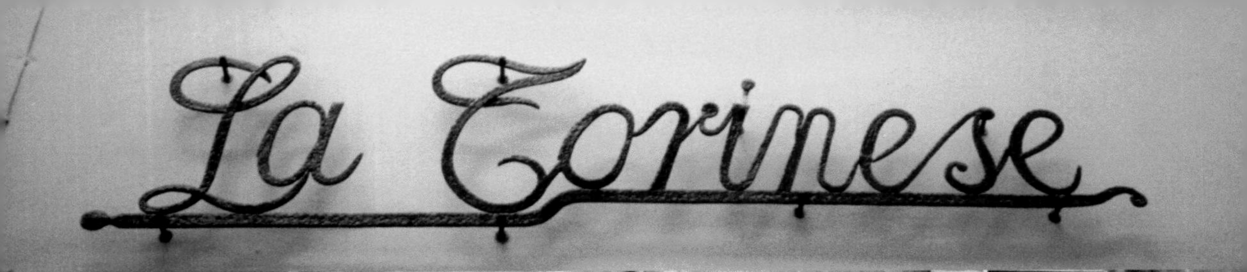
La Torinese

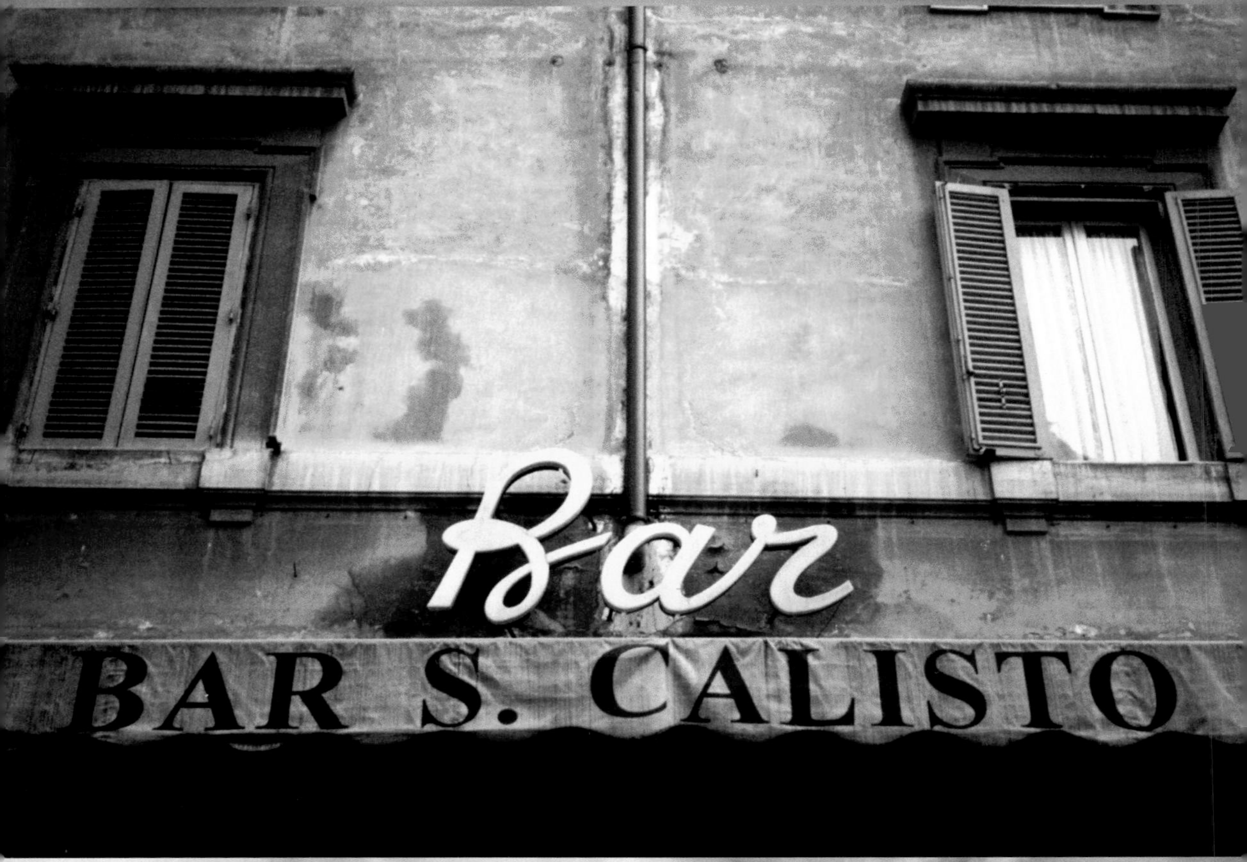
Bar
BAR S. CALISTO

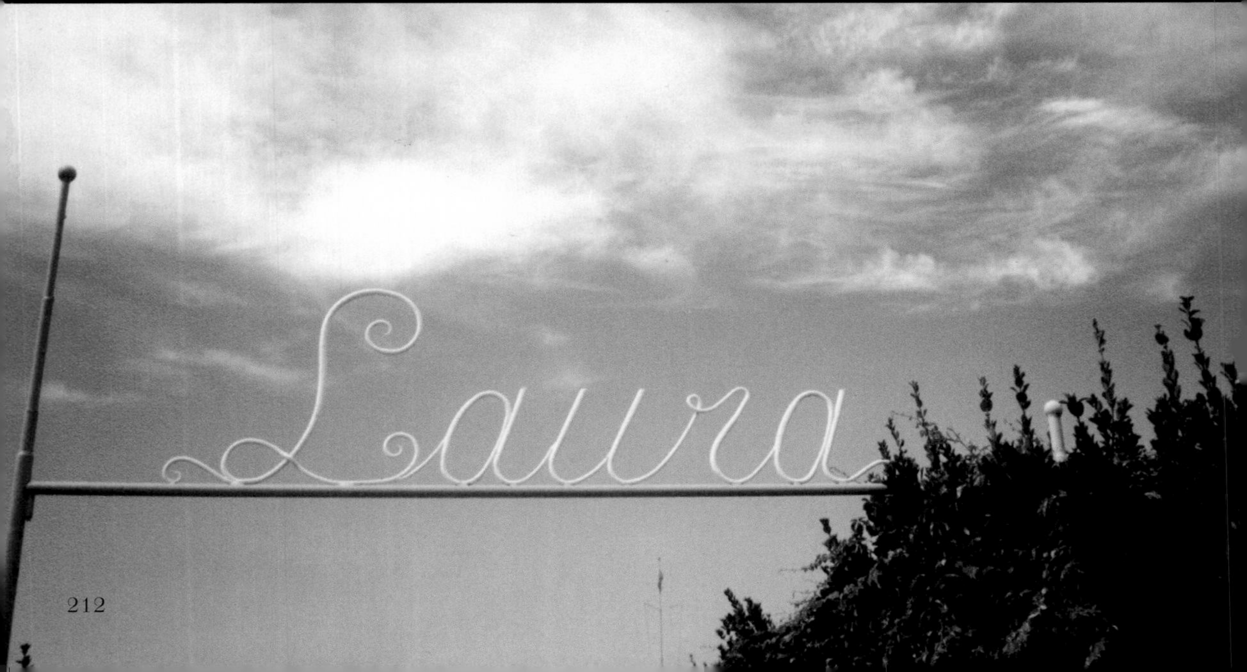
Laura

Castroni

L' Atelier del Gioiello

Bertuccelli

BISELLO VITTORIO
Mercerie

Bar

Tintoria

Bomboniere

Provinciali

Provinciali

1896
Circolo Tennis
Viareggio

Tagliavini

Buon Natale

L'ORIGINALE
Alfredo
RISTORANTE
A 30 METRI

ISTIT
NAZIO
ASSICUR

Al Sogno

Tagliavini

Fioreria

Pescheria
Adriatica

Fior di salute

Barbiere

Auditorium
A.S.A.M

rattoria

Aquisti

30

Capranichetta

Plaza

Dr Chiaro

Calzature

Mancinell

farmacia

RISTORANTE

re degli Amici

Antonella

1889

Trattoria

antica

Carbonara

Gelateria

Salsamenteria

...neabili
...retti

...RTE N. 12.

Tende da Campo
e Sport

il brivido

XVI - Num. 5 - Cent. 50

o corrente postale numero 8.747

PUBBLICITÀ - Per mm. d'altezza (larghezza una colonna): Commerciale L. 4 - Finanziaria L. 5 - Necrologie L. 4
Rubriche: (Echi, Culle, Nozze, Nomine ecc.) L. 7 - Tasse governative in più. Rivolgersi esclusivamente alla
UNIONE PUBBLICITÀ ITALIANA S. A. BOLOGNA, Via Indipendenza 12-14 p. 5. telefono 26-903 e sue succursali

Sett
"IL RESTO

IL GIALLO... E L'AMARANTO

l Livorno scher

re son le cose...

Nuovo ordi
all'Europa sport

tre le cose...
iamo dire, sono tre le squa-
e danno particolare tono e
a momento del Campionato.
pionato che è in marcia da
o giorni. Sono, il Livorno, la
e il Torino. Non chiedete
perchè: tutti lo sappiamo
lo sanno. Vedete il Livor-
corre pancia a terra e non
a indietro: è un episodio ine-
he interessa ed appassiona
e soprattutto per la sua no-

Sotto a chi tocca

a minga? dicono, ma resta
rsi. Anche domenica ha fat-
ose in grande. Bergamo? A
? Sì, lo sappiamo, non si
a di una tappa impossibile.
are, la sostanza relativa del-
cenda diviene materia di po-
giudizio quando si pensi ai
benedetti labronici, mai vi-
A tanto baldanzosi e tanto
ualità come in questo mo-
avevano pur fatto qualcosa
to analogo (ed in epoca non
ntemente remota per scor-
in quel di Torino, dove un
sta portando sulla scena
ari di illustrissime vittime.
Livorno, insomma, dimostra
erci fare e bene. Che sia la
ra nuova che sta venendo a
Che voglia proprio essere
lieta sorpresa del terzo
ionato di guerra? La rispo-
balza da una domenica al-
Torino diede l'allarme:
di paglia, si disse... vedremo
Ora, sotto a chi tocca. Il

devole: niente di niente. Torino-
Genova di domenica è un brillante episodio sportivo che onora in
eguale misura tutti i suoi prota-
gonisti.
E il Toro ha vinto un'altra volta e fa dell'altra strada. L'insegui-
mento è iniziato e per il momento
ha uno sviluppo calmo, regolare e
positivo. Si salvi chi può... Senza
scherzi, si ha la sensazione che i
granata stiano mettendosi definiti-
vamente a posto e che debbano ar-
rivare lontano, molto lontano. Come si è sempre ritenuto, del resto.
Lo dice il rendimento della squa-
dra e lo dicono il rendimento degli uomini: la forma sembra vol-
stia « scoppiando » in pieno nei
ranghi granata, se è vero che si
esalta oggi chi appena due setti-
mane fa era giudicato fermo e che
la geniale azione delle pedine sin-
gole si traduce nel magistrale tono
di tutta la unità. Cento motivi,
forse, concorrono a spiegare la re-
pentina quanto formidabile ripre-
sa torinese. Ma, certo, vi ha con-
tribuito anche il sistema che ha
fissato compiti precisi per ogni a-
tleta, che ha permesso al reparto
d'attacco di svolgere una più aperta manovra, che ha creato un tra-
pezio centrale e in grado di co-
mandare il giuoco.
L'occasione ci fornisce lo spunto
per rilevare che la questione del
sistema è generalmente ora giudi-
cata con maggiore serenità e paca-
tezza, il che, contrariamente a

quanto avvenne nel passato, finirà
forse per incoraggiare le squadre
che, con ragione e base, o meno,
vorranno tentare la nuova tattica
per farsi un'esperienza di più.

Gioie e dolori

Beh, lasciamo il sistema e tor-
niamo al Campionato. Il primo
successo del Vicenza coincide col
primo sbaglio della Triestina. Ma,
sentite: Colaussi e Benigni, lan-
ciati da Quaresima, hanno fatto
cose egregie, operando alle loro
spalle la famosa mediana al com-
pleto Fattori, Santagiuliana, Abe-
ni che ben conosciamo; e la Triestina si è battuta con cuore e spin-
ta fino all'ultimo, rasentando più
volte il pareggio. In breve, premio
e incoraggiamento per il Vicenza
che ha vinto su di una Triestina
sempre brillante ma sfortu-
nata.
Anche il Liguria ha fatto per la
prima volta bottino intero, colpen-
do una Juventus che deve avere
risentito alquanto della mancanza
del suo regista di sistema, in una
fase per essa tanto delicata.
Giornata scarsa, molto scarsa,
del Milano, allineatosi con un por-
tiere novellino ed emozionato, e-
però inevitabilmente incassatore,
ma giornata di grazia della Fiorentina, una Fiorentina che si rive-
la in pieno, che giuoco, manovra
con arte e corre decisamente a
bersaglio. Non è la prima volta
che la Fiorentina indovina la grande partita a Milano; codesta sua
affermazione ha però il tono di
quelle che dicono e svelano, quan-

*Tutti i veri sportivi sanno,
meno dovrebbero sapere, ch
qualche tempo ci sono degli
ni in Italia e in Germania ch
vorano per la riorganizzazione
lo sport europeo, ma non tutt
se si rendono conto dell'impo
za di tale opera, delle sue rag
dei suoi scopi.*

*Bisogna sapere quale fos
situazione allorché il C.O.N.
dirigenti dello sport germa
decisero ad affrontare e a ris
il problema della organizza
sportiva internazionale. Cias
attività sportiva faceva cap
una Federazione o Associazio
ternazionale perfettamente or
zata e perfettamente funzio
dal punto di vista formale, m
rimediabilmente viziata in
punti sostanziali della sua st
ra. Precisamente:*

*1) Nel sistema di delibera
fondato sulla votazione, perc
ciascuna Nazione era asse
un numero di voti differente
che quello spettante alle N
anglosassoni (Inghilterra, U
Australia ecc.) fosse in ogni
superiore a quello spettante
te le altre Nazioni messe ins

*2) Negli orientamenti tec
organizzativi perchè essi ven
rigorosamente mantenuti qu
rano al momento della cre
dell'Ente Internazionale
quindici, venti anni fa.*

*Porre fine a questo stato
dal quale veniva un danno
inceppamento al movimento s*

e de "..CARLINO ,, | DIREZIONE E AMMIN: VIA DOGALI, 5 - BOLOGNA | Abbonamenti | Italia - Impero - Colonie L. 22 / Estero . . . . . . 38 / Estero ogni numero cent. 75 | Mercoledì 28 ottobre 194.
Telefoni: 33-810 - 33-819 - 20-334 - 28-128 - 23-201 | Sped. in abbonamento postale - secondo

EL CAMPIONATO DI CALCIO

a o fa sul serio"

Il "Toro,, infuria   infila il "Grifo

TORINO. 27 — Tripudio di ven-
mila tifosi, domenica, sul campo
l Torino (gli altri che contribui-
no a gremire ogni ordine di
ano juventini o genoves
vano seguito la sua
con una tacit
eranza ch
pu
attu
nat
uadr
Erano
«5 a
o Stadi
nti speci
attacco
sta "conval
o, e un'a
la prima
rte di due ali e
ale che se la in
artite (sia pure c
usori avversari) »,
«Toro» ha
bbi sulla sua eff
ssistere, giocando u
quale non c'è che da
i cappello (chi ha
i i novanta minuti
comandato il giuoc
Erano rimasti alcuni du
«5 a 2» della domenic
o Stadio Mussolini, dubb
nti specialmente la difesa
— si diceva — è fronte
attacco un po' a pezzi, co
"convalescente e un Me
rmo, e un'altra avere a
la prima linea del Geno
di due ali sfolgoranti co
onti e Neri e di un terzetto ce
se la intende e meravigli

Bisogn
situa

fiorellini

233

148. Label for Acqua di Colonia (eau de Cologne), 1912.

149. Brand-name customized script for Larius pen points, *c.* 1925.

150–51. Letter- and billheads in various engraver's scripts, 1884–1900.

152–53. Billhead for Michele Franco, jeweler, Turin, using various engraver's scripts (and cursive handwriting), 1893.

154–55. Billhead from a French dress shop in Turin, 1895.

156–57. Billhead from an upholsterer in Bellagio, 1900.

158–59. Billhead from a laundry in Turin, 1895.

160–61. Billheads from a florist and a hat shop, 1891 and 1918.

162–63. Billhead from a lingerie shop in Turin, 1888.

164–65. Billhead from a glassworks in Modena, 1944.

166. Official notice of distinction from King Vittorio Emanuele III, employing various scripts, 1924.

167. Printer's letterpress proof of a business card for Mario Mosca, *c.* 1925.

168–69. Specimen of Serie Remo script from *Campionario Caratteri e Fregi Tipografici*, Ditta Nebiolo & Comp., Turin, 1918, Italy's most famous type foundry.

170. Masthead from *Excelsior* magazine, 1926.

171. Customized lettering from an issue of *Le Grandi Firme* magazine, date unknown.

172–73. Masthead from *La Donna Fascista*, a Fascist party women's journal, 1940.

174. Script that mimics thread used to advertise fabrics, *c.* 1930.

175. Script that mimics handwriting, used on a sentimental postcard. *c.* 1920.

176. Customized script for Rem brand, for a suit manufacturer, *c.* 1930.

177. 'Perfume script' for Coty perfume advertisement, 1951.

178. Outline script masthead for *Il Dramma* magazine, 1934.

179. Distinctive masthead for *Le Grandi Firme*, edited by Pitigrilli (who is credited with designing the magazine), 1934.

180–81. Packaging proof for Bergamotto toothpaste, with customized script brand name, 1952.

182. Sheet music for *Mélodies* by F. Paolo Tosti, with Art Nouveau-inspired lettering, *c.* 1910.

183. Cover of *Campionario Caratteri e Fregi Tipografici*, Ditta Nebiolo & Comp., Turin, 1918.

184. Masthead for *Il Secolo Illustrato* with cover illustration by Marcello Dudovich, 1918.

185. Masthead for *Lo Sport Illustrato e la Guerra*, combining sports with World War I, 1916.

186–89. Pages from the textbook *Sillabario e Piccole Letture*, published by La Libreria dello Stato, Rome, 1931.

190–91. Specimens of Bastarda Filettata and Scrittura Italica from *Campionario Caratteri e Fregi Tipografici*, Ditta Nebiolo & Comp., Turin, Italy, 1918.

192–93. Specimens of Caratteri Manoscritto and Scrittura Verticale from *Campionario Caratteri e Fregi Tipografici*, Ditta Nebiolo & Comp., Turin, Italy, 1918.

194–95. Specimens of Scrittura Inglese and Scrittura Inglese Neretta from *Campionario Caratteri e Fregi Tipografici*, Ditta Nebiolo & Comp., Turin, Italy, 1918.

196–97. Specimens of Scrittura Bastarda, Chiara, and Scrittura Americana from *Campionario Caratteri e Fregi Tipografici*, Ditta Nebiolo & Comp., Turin, Italy, 1918. (Note: this face in France is called Ecriture Parisienne.)

198–99. Specimens of Serie Gloria and Corsivi Réclame from *Campionario Caratteri e Fregi Tipografici*, Ditta Nebiolo & Comp., Turin, Italy, 1918.

200–1. Letterhead for Cooperativa Produttori Ortaggi e Frutta, fruit and vegetable vendor, 1926. (inset) Label for Arancio, orange juice, *c.* 1950.

202–3. Various wine labels, 1950s.

204–5. Labels for fruit syrups with customized scripts indicating the flavors, 1923.

206–9. Poetic handwriting in a student's *quaderno* (notebook), 1923. (inset, right) Packages for flower-scented toilet powder, *c.* 1930. (inset, left) Paesaggio colored pencils, *c.* 1950.

210–11. *Corso di Bella Scrittura*, a handwriting exercise book for children, 1949.

212–23. Various commercial store signs from Florence, Lucca, Venice, and Rome (photographs by Louise Fili).

224–25. Customized lettering for Perugina confectionery tin, 1933.

226–27. Customized outline script, influenced by Stile Liberty, for an umbrella manufacturer, 1908.

228–29. Customized lettering influenced by the flowing ribbon on the tin for baby food, 1940s.

230–31. Masthead for *Il Brivido Sportivo*, a sports newspaper, 1942. (inset) Packaging for talcum powder.

232–33. Shadowed outline script for the brand name on a confectionery tin, 1940s.

American

'RITING IS IN THE MIDDLE OF THE FAMOUS THREE Rs— READING, 'RITING, 'RITHMETIC—AND CURSIVE SCRIPT has been the standard form of 'riting in schools since the mid-19th century. It has been rigorously taught in various ways: the most common are the methods known as Spencerian, Zaner-Bloser, Palmer, and, to a lesser extent, D'Nealian. Time was when anxious school-children were forced to hold their pens in a particular manner in order to write the right way (and preferably with the right hand), ensuring that the little cursive tails neatly connected to the adjacent ones.

The most commonly practiced method was Spencerian, created by Platt Rogers Spencer. In 1840, Spencer developed a method that enabled penmanship to be practiced quickly and legibly, with decided panache. In the latter part of the 19th century his method was improved by adjusting the mechanics of writing and renamed "The New Spencerian." The hypnotic procedure of making all the letters of the alphabet form sinuous curves and bold perpendicular lines was considered the epitome of personal and business penmanship. Spencerian is, therefore, the basis for many American script typefaces, and was the inspiration for such logos as Coca Cola, Pepsi Cola and Ford Motor Company, as well as many others made obsolete long ago. Spencerian is much too fussy for the computer age.

The easier Palmer Method, conceived in the late 19th century by Austin Norman Palmer, who edited *The American Penman* magazine, demanded an equally rhythmic hand motion, although the end results were much less ornate. In fact, flourishes were forcefully discouraged. Palmer's *Guide to Business Writing* (1894) sold over one million copies and his handwriting charts were in almost every American classroom.

The Zaner method was created in 1888 by Charles Paxton Zaner who founded the Zanerian College of Penmanship in Columbus, Ohio. Its aim was to prepare young penmen for the transcription of official documents used by businesses. The typewriter, its design standardized by 1910, duly eliminated the need for these industrial-age scribes, and Zaner's method was redirected towards children. Lastly, D'Nealian, developed by Donald Thurber in 1978, had some success and is still taught.

While handwriting methods definitely influenced the fundamentals of script typefaces, type designers and sign painters took the art of cursive letter-writing to much more ambitious heights. Lettering in the United States did not have the same history as in Europe, where advertising was more of a soft sell. American scripts were intended to grab the eye, and certain conventions grew and reinforced this aim.

American output was not, however, inferior or poor. The trademarks for Blum & Rubenoffs Woolens, Charles Roland Bakery and Royal Hudson's Obesity Oil (pp. 336–37) are as beautifully intricate as any Victorian-style engraved scripts. Although they looked similar, these marks were typographically demonstrative—and visually eye-catching.

Scripts were used more for novelty than for elegance. Novelty Script, for example, is a precisionist brush script that borrows from both handwriting and the comic typeface Bamboo. Yet it has a curious appeal by virtue of the rhythmic way the capitals harmonize with the lower case. Likewise, the tightly condensed Shepard Script Series (p. 323), a Spencerian script on steroids, also moves rhythmically like a page of musical notation.

The most iconic American scripts were late 19th- and early 20th-century cigar labels (pp. 282–87), which adopted the Victorian era's ornamented borders and bifurcated circus lettering. Made as scripts, these complex branding devices were like typographical sculptures.

Scripts were used in the United States for a slew of everyday printing needs—from social printing (invitations and certificates) to advertisements for Kleaner Sanitowels, Regal Millinery, Mattson High School (pp. 302–3), Eagle Aircraft Corporation, and Emerson Hats (pp. 306–7). Usually, scripts were decided upon by a commercial printer, whose stock of fonts determined which faces would be pushed to the customer. Scripts were selected over Roman typefaces because they offered a more dynamic, forward-thrusting, kinetic sensibility. But also in the case of brush or nib-pen scripts, a personal, signature-like effect was prevalent.

Good aesthetics were useful, too. Or as one printing specimen sheet declared in a headline, albeit in a rather strange construction: "It pays to look well." Scripts made "well" into a fine art. ❧

CHINA
CRYSTAL

artin's

SILVER
ANTIQUES

Ribbon

Rope

Ribbon

Ribbon

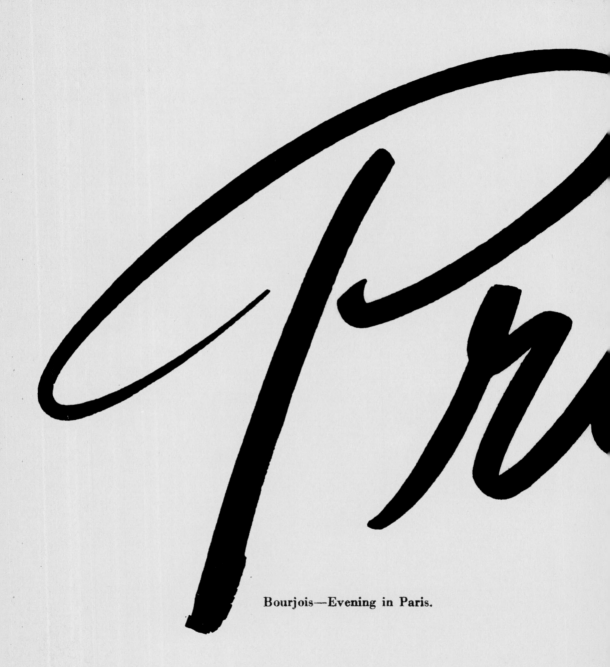

Bourjois—Evening in Paris.

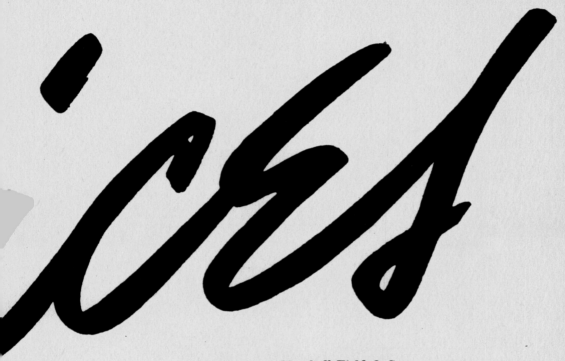

Marshall Field & Co.

Winsor & Newton No. 3
Series 7 Sable Hair No. 5

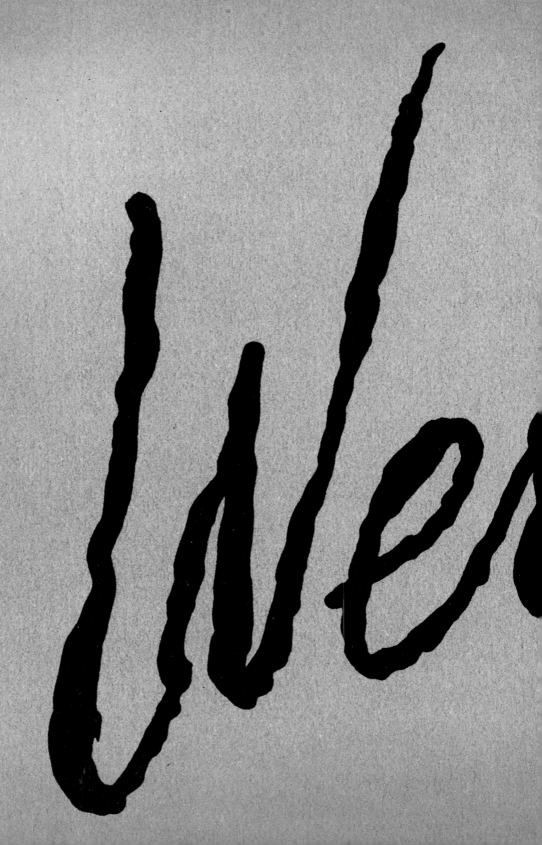

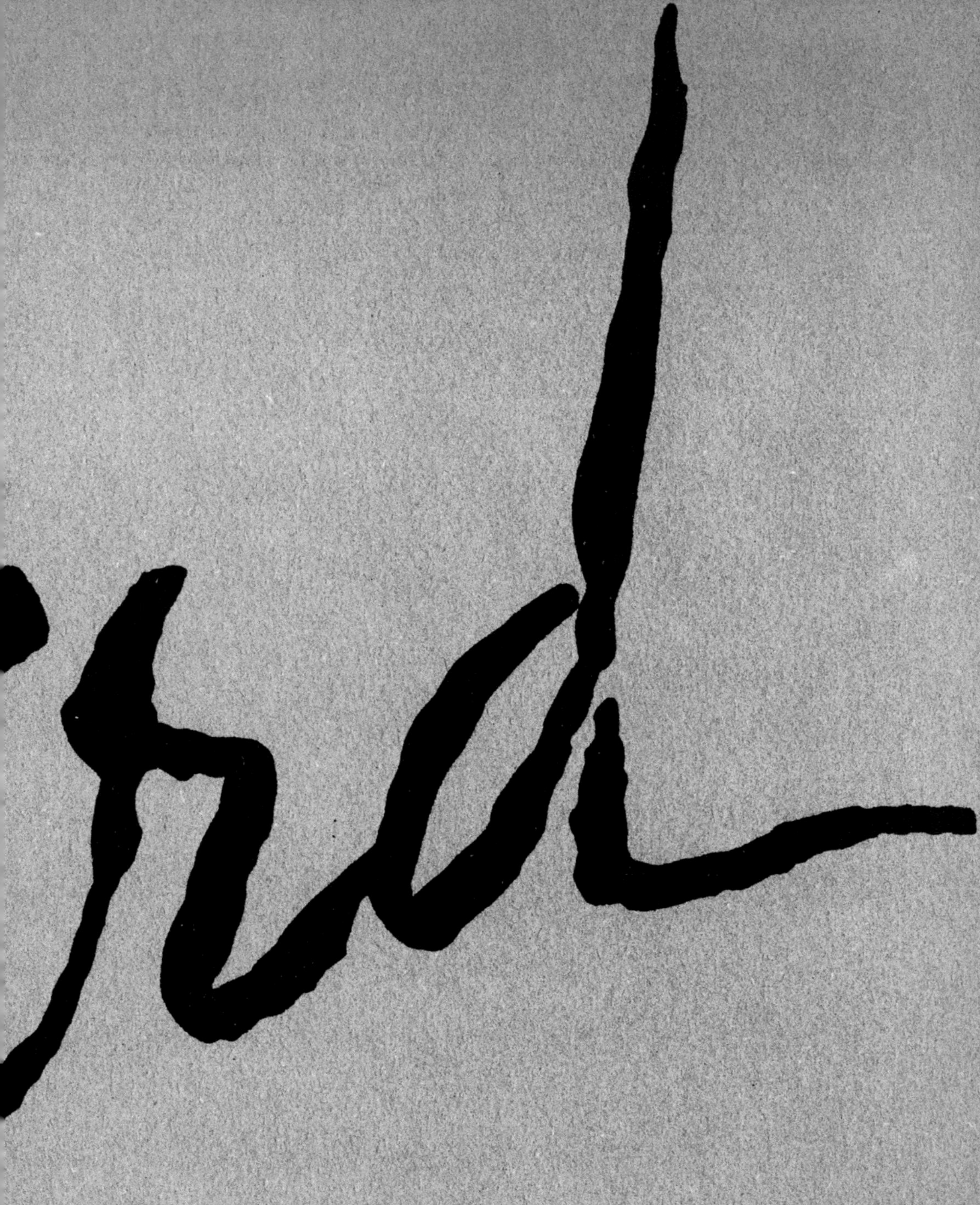

Mar

a "handwritten"

informal adve

date

' typeface for

tising display

A B C D E F G H I J K L M N O P Q R S T...

a b c d e f g h i j k l m n o p q r s t u v w x y z   1 2 3 4 5 6 7 8 9 0 $

The Romance of Capri

24 point large   no. 30 46 24   4×A 13×a 9×1

Glassware an

Leonardo da Vinci

30 point   no. 30 46 28   4×A 11×a 7×1

New Y

Modern Hats

36 point   no. 30 46 36   3×A 9×a 5×1

Wild

Old Art

48 point   no. 30 46 48   3×A 6×a 4×1

Elega

Sunshine

60 point   no. 30 46 60   3×A 5×a 3×1

Per

Distributed by:

Amsterdam Continental Types   *and Graphic Equipm*

268-276 Fourth Avenue, New York 10, N. Y.,   Telephone: SPring 7-4980

Porcelain

Show

Clowers

ce

ume

Boulevard

Calligraphic elegance in the English style. The

12 point   no. 30 46 12   9 × A 39 × a 14 × 1

Ideal Script for private printed matters,

14 point   no. 30 46 14   9 × A 34 × a 14 × 1

Display work, and catalogues. With

18 point   no. 30 46 16   6 × A 24 × a 12 × 1

Modern caps and swing letters

24 point small   no. 30 46 20   5 × A 18 × a 9 × 1

Inc.

ABCDEFGHIJKLMNOPQQ
WXYZ abcdefghijklmnopqrstuvwxyz 1

Holidays in Florida

30 point   no. 38 44 51   5×A 16×a 8×1

Dancing-Party

36 point   no. 38 44 52   5×A 12×a 7×1

New Garden

48 point   no. 38 44 53   4×A 10×a 5×1

Jazzband

72 point small   no. 38 44 54   4×A 8×a 4×1

Excellent

72 point large   no. 38 44 55   3×A 6×a 4×1

Vins Liq

Black a

Rege

Me

Cro

Distributed by :

Amsterdam Continental Types and Graphic Equipm

252

268-276 Fourth Avenue, New York 10, N.Y., Telephone: Spring 7-4980

s Drinks

White

Bar

opol

tion

An attractive Creation

More than a mere Type ... it means Delicacy!

12 point　no. 38 44 46　　11 × A 48 × a 15 × 1

Incomparable Crispness and Smartness

14 point　no. 38 44 47　　9 × A 40 × a 13 × 1

Winged like steps of a whirling dance

18 point　no. 38 44 48　　7 × A 32 × a 12 × 1

A lovely script. Non-kerning

24 point small　no. 38 44 49　　5 × A 22 × a 10 × 1

Design of special variability

24 point large　no. 38 44 50　　5 × A 20 × a 9 × 1

Inc.,

Send for specimens of other BERTHOLD type faces

A B C D E F
a b c d e f g h i

Moder

Publ

Jaz

Tob

Reiner Black

An attractive display type face

14 point   no. 30 48 14   12×A 24×a 10×1

Of highly impressive forms, a

18 point   no. 30 48 16   9×A 20×a 9×1

Masterly design by the

24 point small   no. 30 48 20   7×A 12×a 7×1

Artist Imre Reiner

24 point large   no. 30 48 24   6×A 11×a 7×1

Distributed by:

Amsterdam Continental Types   *and Graphic Equip*

268-276 Fourth Avenue, New York 10, N. Y.,   Telephone: SPring 7-4980

254

HIJKLMNOPQRSTUVWXYZ

lmnopqrstuvwxyz 1234567890 $

Printers

New Advertising

30 point   no. 30 48 28   5×A 9×a 5×1

ations

GardenBook

36 point   no. 30 48 36   4×A 7×a 4×1

Club

Old River

48 point   no. 30 48 48   3×A 6×a 4×1

acco

Albany

60 point   no. 30 48 60   3×A 5×a 3×1

Inc.

Send for specimens of other BERTHOLD type faces

Silence is a great peacemaker

Silence is a great peacemaker

Silence is a great peacemaker

Silence is a great peacemaker

Silence is a great peacemaker

Silence is a great peacemaker

Silence is a great peacemaker

Silence is a great peacemaker

Silence is a great peacemaker

Silence is a great peacemaker

Silence is a great peacemaker

Silence is a great peacemaker

Silence is a great peacemaker

Silence is a great peacemaker

Silence is a great peacemaker

Silence is a great peacemaker

Silence is a great peacemaker

Silence is a great peacemaker

Silence is a great peacemaker

Silence is a great peacemaker

Silence is a great peacemaker

Silence is a great peacemaker

Silence is a great peacemaker

Silence is a great peacemaker

A Showing of
The New Civilité
Type Series

American Type Founders Company
Sets the Type Fashions

Civilite

Being a Present-day Interpretation
of the Quaint Charm of the Writing of the Sixteenth
Century Calligraphers, Freely Rendered,
with an Eye to Legibility
and Usefulness

48 Point   4 A $6 50 12 a $7 25 $13 75

French Bibliophile
Private Library Sales

36 Point   5 A $5 25 15 a $6 00 $11 25

Bookplate Exhibitions
Restores Illuminated Manuscript

30 Point   6 A $4 55 18 a $4 70 $9 25

Print Collectors form Society
Type Designs Adapted to Modern Use

24 Point   8 A $4 00 24 a $4 50 $8 50

Copperplate Engravings Admired
Used Lavishly by Eighteenth Century Printers

18 Point   10 A $3 00 30 a $3 25 $6 25   12 Point   15 A $2 40 45 a $2 75 $5 15

Artistic French Etching   Old Type Faces Revived
Well Proportioned Title Pages   Publishers Announce Competitions
                                        First Colonial Printers

A B C D E E F
G H H I J K K
L M N N O P Q
R S T U V W
X Y Z & ~ ∾

$ 1 2 3 4 5 6 7 8 9 0

a a b c d d ɛ e e f
g g ɦ ħ i j k l l m m
n n o p p q r s s
t t u v v w x y z

nd ge . . , ~ ' ' : ; ! ?

Leading printers and designers are using Trafton Script daily because they have found it an effective sales stimulator — a dependable typographic tool for

Printing Success.
Here are just a few suggestions for using Trafton Script in ways which assure profits, and the good-will of your customers:

Greetings and Invitations.
Trafton Script is an ideal type choice for "plateless engraving", raised letters, greeting cards, invitations, and all types of personal printing forms. It creates an individual atmosphere.

House Organs.
Have you a House Organ that needs re-dressing and styling up? If so, you'll find no type more dashing, elegant, and distinctive than Trafton Script.

Booklets and Folders.
All direct-mail folders and booklets face tremendous competition for attention. Trafton Script helps you produce sales literature that will escape the wastebasket.

Window Display Cards
must fulfill a double function. They must be attractive enough to help the appearance of the windows in which they appear, and they must SELL MERCHANDISE! Trafton Script has proved its effectiveness on both counts in actual use in the largest stores in the country.

Stationery
must express the personality of the sender. Leading advertisers have proved the effectiveness of Trafton Script for letter-heads used in direct-mail campaigns. It lends fresh charm to personal letterheads, too.

Wine—Lists and Menus
are assuming new importance in these post-prohibition days. Trafton Script banishes that stodgy conventional look — it imbues wine-lists and menus with a grace and spontaneity — appropriate to the noble art of dining.

14 Point 9 A 36 a

Bauer, presen
leads the fiel

16 Point 8 A 28 a

Flowing and
will find mar

18 Point 7 A 24 a

With the c
the first flo

60 Point 3 A 10 a

D

72 Point 3 A 8 a

Jour

84 Point 3 A 5 a

Na

𝒴 𝒥 &

this excellent type face, again
. A. Trafton, the American

amic commercial typography
possibilities in this excellent

etion of the foundation
ams are placed. Almost

Selection from the great Masters

Concert in the Lincoln Park

Graphic Arts Exposition

The beautiful Book

tinguished Earl of Stratford

eys to South America

ional Music Hall

Per set, one each, $4.95 | Single character 50c   Cast in type molds on regular body, not recessed

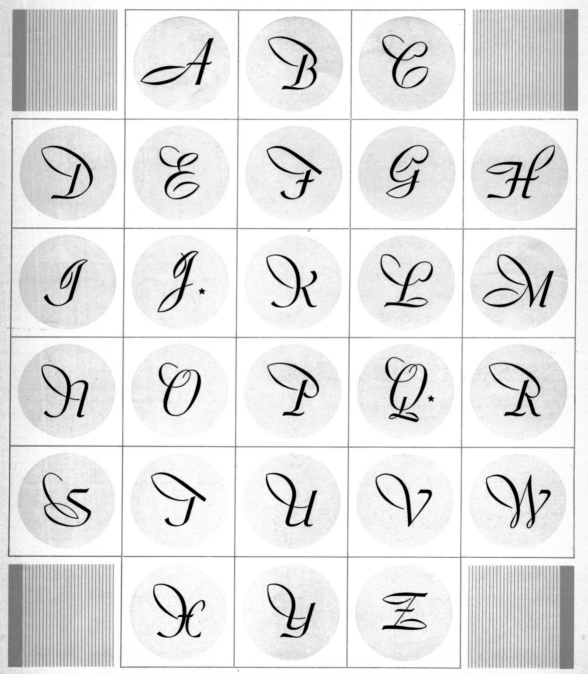

★ Initials J and Q cast on 60-point body

Raleigh Initials will also be obtainable in other sizes
Ask for complete showing

36 Point

A B C
D E F G
H I J K
L M N O
P Q R S
T U V W
X Y Z

Initials J and Q cast on size larger body
26 characters made in all sizes

96 Point

C E D

84 Point

B H F

72 Point

L M G J

60 Point

A Y O P I

54 Point

M Q R A S

48 Point

G T U X V Z

36 Point

M K L J D R H

An Exhibition

OF SCULPTURE BY REUBEN HALS,

CALLED THE RACE OF MAN, WILL

BE OPENED TO THE PUBLIC FROM

FEBRUARY SECOND TO TWELFTH

AT THE MOLIERE ART GALLERIES

Raleigh Cursive

72 Point

Bright Star

60 Point

Yellow Gown

48 Point

Respectfully
Superior Quality

42 Point

Cosmopolitan
Flourishing Garden

36 Point

Historical Book
Reliable Encyclopedia

30 Point

Delightful Entertainment
Professional Talent

24 Point

Excellent Symphony Orchestra
Sixteenth Anniversary

18 Point

College Diplomas
Stationery

14 Point

Bewildering Loveliness
Hairdressing

12 Point

Unique Creations
Gold Certificate Bought
Reorganization

10 Point

Admirable Color Scheme
Introduces New Automobile
Luxurious Homes

Characters in Complete Font

A B C D E F G
H I J K L M N
O P Q R S T U
V W X Y Z & $
1 2 3 4 5 6 7 8 9 0
a b c d e f g h i j k l m
n o p q r s t u v w x y z
ar er ir as es is us . , - ' ' : ; ! ?

Prices and Schemes of Job Fonts

72 Point	Caps 3A $10 90	Lowercase 4a $5 75	Points $1 30	Figures $2 60	Total $20 55			
60 Point	Caps 4A 9 05	Lowercase 7a 6 60	Points 1 15	Figures 2 30	Total 19 10			
48 Point	Caps 5A 7 60	Lowercase 10a 5 15	Points 95	Figures 1 90	Total 15 60			
42 Point	Caps 6A 7 45	Lowercase 11a 5 25	Points 85	Figures 1 70	Total 15 25			
36 Point	Caps 6A 5 75	Lowercase 11a 4 30	Points 75	Figures 1 50	Total 12 30			
30 Point	Caps 7A 4 55	Lowercase 13a 3 40	Points 65	Figures 1 30	Total 9 90			
24 Point	Caps 9A 3 75	Lowercase 18a 3 20	Points 55	Figures 1 10	Total 8 60			
18 Point	Caps 15A $4 00	Lowercase 28a $2 80	Total $6 80					
14 Point	Caps 21A 3 75	Lowercase 41a 2 55	Total 6 30					
12 Point	Caps 22A 3 35	Lowercase 45a 2 45	Total 5 80					
10 Point	Caps 27A 2 95	Lowercase 55a 2 25	Total 5 20					

10 to 18 point sizes of Raleigh Cursive are cast only on
the regular straight body

Complete angle body fonts, in sizes 24 to 72 point, will come to you in parcels as follows:
Caps A to Z & — Lowercase a to z — Figures 1 to 0 $—Points . , - ' ' : ; ! ?

Bristol

A NEW DEAL IN
HOTELS

RALEIGH INITIAL   RALEIGH CURSIVE AND STYMIE LIGHT

Characters

A B C D E F G H
I J K L M N O
P Q R S T U
V W X Y Z & $
a b c d e f g h i j k l m
n o p q r s t u v w x y z
ar er ir as es is us . , - ' ' : ; ! ?
1 2 3 4 5 6 7 8 9 0

72 Point   3A 4a

Highest Realm

60 Point   4A 7a

Magnificent Gowns

48 Point   5A 10a

Enterprising Diplomatist

42 Point   6A 11a

Bulgaria Imported Biplanes

36 Point   6A 11a

Delightful Saxophone Orchestra

30 Point   7A 13a

Noted Educator Attending Convention

24 Point   9A 18a

Beautiful Women Handsomely Gowned

18 Point   15A 28a

Typographic Specimen Deserved Honorable Mention

14 Point   21A 41a

Recent Developments in Horticulture Exciting Considerable Interest

12 Point   22A 45a

Wonderful Reception Tendered International Heroes During Celebration

10 Point   27A 55a

Exhibition of Rare Curios and Fine Antiques Continues to Attract Notable Connoisseurs

Sizes 24 to 72 Point cast on Angle Body

Weights and Prices given are Approximate; see page 2.   Cast on Text Line.

8 A 25 a   14 Point Lining Plate Script No. 2   3⁵⁄₁₆ lbs., **$3.75**

Mid-Winter Singing and Dancing Classes Will Open

The First of December With An Entirely New List of Teachers

1234567890

7 A 21 a   18 Point Lining Plate Script No. 2   4½ lbs., **$4.50**

Attend Our Grand Annual Fall Opening of

Gents Ready-to-wear 916 Trousers, Suits and Overcoats

5 A 16 a   24 Point Lining Plate Script No. 2   5⁹⁄₁₆ lbs., **$5.00**

Handsome Wedding Announcements

Executed With Our 542 Popular Plate Scripts

4 A 13 a   36 Point Lining Plate Script No. 2   7¹⁵⁄₁₆ lbs., **$6.50**

Southwestern Associations

Meetings Start 95 First of October

3 A 9 a   48 Point Lining Plate Script No. 2   10⅜ lbs., **$7.50**

Gorgeous Apartments

Traveler 23 European Hotel

Mr. and Mrs. Sidney Miller

request the honor of your presence at the

marriage of their daughter

Lura Adena

and

Mr. Gerald Ewing Young

on the evening of Wednesday June the eighth

nineteen hundred and eight at

six o'clock sharp

785 South Burnside Street

Chicago

POINT-LINE, POINT-SET, POINT-BODY   QUALITY AND FINISH UNEQUALED

Weights and Prices given are Approximate; see page 2.   Cast on Text Line.

5 A 15 a   30 Point Lining Grace Script No. 1   6⅜ lbs., $5.50

Lillian Montrose Honors Her Friends

With an Invitation to Her Afternoon Receptions

1234567890

4 A 12 a   30 Point Lining Grace Script No. 2   6⅜ lbs., $5.50

Delicate Effects in Waist Goods

Elegant Displays 62 in Our Windows

Yourself and friends are invited to attend a

Banquet and Ball

given by

The Grace Script Club

Thursday evening February Seventeenth

nineteen hundred and eight

Aaa Bbb

Eef Fff Gg

Kkk Lll Mm

Qqu Rrr Sss

Ww Xx

More Profits 17

72 Point Ludlow 36-BIC Mandate

A Pleasing New Face 25
In the morning editions

48 Point Ludlow 36-BIC Mandate

Satisfied Users Demand This 49
Face to lend ads an informal tone

36 Point Ludlow 36-BIC Mandate

This Dynamic Face is the Latest Creation in 36
A script type providing variety in display matter

24 Point Ludlow 36-BIC Mandate

Characters in Complete Font

A B C D E F G H I J K L M N O P Q
R S T U V W X Y Z & $ 1 2 3 4 5 6 7 8 9 0
a b c d e f g h i j k l m n o p q r s t u v
w x y z . : , ; - — ' ' ! ? ( ) [ ] of on or 's

Check These Points

Will these Ludlow features improve the showing... ing room with respect to economy and efficiency?

Because, with the Ludlow, a slugline is produced direct from the copy, all expense of sorts casting or type replenishment is eliminated.	
There being no type to deal with in advance of productive composition, the Ludlow system eliminates all expense for storage, case inspection, and case laying.	
The use of the Ludlow for display gives you the inestimable advantage of all-slug make-up.	
A change-over to the Ludlow system of display composition makes an important saving in the floor space required for display composition.	
With the Ludlow every issue contains only new and unbroken typefaces, italic as well as roman.	

There are many other Ludlow advantages which will repay investigation. We repeat: The Ludlow provides flexibility—efficiently. Its simplicity in operation and mechanism permits the compositor to concentrate all his attention on composition.

LUDLOW TYPOGRAPH COMPANY
2032 CLYBOURN AVENUE
CHICAGO, ILLINOIS

Set in the Ludlow Tempo family

no. 584 446   12 point
11 × A   48 × a   15 × 1   1 fount about 4 lbs

New Models from the Spring Collections of some famous Dress Des

no. 584 447   14 point
9 × A   42 × a   13 × 1   1 fount about 4.66 lbs.

Made in England especially for Asprey & Co. 1234567

no. 584 448   18 point
7 × A   32 × a   12 × 1   1 fount about 5.32 lbs.

Unquestionably the Finest Whisky Scotland Prodi

no. 584 449   24 point small
5 × A   22 × a   10 × 1   1 fount about 6.51 lbs

Powder and Mousse Day Cream " Innos

no. 584 450   24 point large
5 × A   20 × a   9 × 1   1 fount about 7 lbs.

Branch of The Imperial Tobacco Birn

no. 584 451   30 point
5 × A   16 × a   8 × 1   1 fount about 10 lbs.

Admired by Lovers of the Beautifi

no. 584 452   36 point
5 × A   12 × a   7 × 1   1 fount about 12.26 lbs

The Highway of Fashio

no. 584 453   48 point
4 × A   10 × a   5 × 1   1 fount about 16.33 lbs.

Symphonic Orchestri

no. 584 454   72 point small
4 × A   8 × a   5 × 1   1 fount about 25 lbs.

Practical Gifts

no. 584 455   72 point large
5 × A   6 × a   5 × 1   1 fount about 25.3 lbs.

White Hall

Aa Bb Cc Dd Ee Ff Gg Hh Ii Jj Kk Ll Mm Nn Oo Pp Quq Rr Ss Tt Th Uu Vv Ww Xx Yy Zz & $ 1234567890 .,. '' :;!? „ »« (–/

The book letter used in this specimen is WALBAUM and WALBAUM ITALIC, one of the finest classic characters in the world, a product of the Berthold Type Foundry, Berlin/Germany.

Signal Medium

Routes to Australia, New Zealand and the Near East, also to Pakistan across the Indian Ocean

no. 384 049   18 point
12×A   24×a   11×1   1 fount about 5,2 lbs.

The famed All-Sleepers Plane to Egypt French Masterpiece from our collection

no. 384 050   24 point small
9×A   16×a   9×1   1 fount about 6,34 lbs.

A land of Sunshine and Sports Yellow Mill, a Name of Quality

no. 384 051   24 point large
8×A   13×a   8×1   1 fount about 6,5 lbs.

That is a business of yours!

no. 384 052   30 point
7×A   11×a   7×1   1 fount about 8,12 lbs.

Dynamic Headphones

no. 384 054   36 point
5×A   9×a   5×1   1 fount about 9,62 lbs.

Winter in Brazil

no. 384 056   48 point
4×A   7×a   4×1   1 fount about 13,22 lbs.

Central Park

no. 384 057   60 point
3×A   5×a   4×1   1 fount about 17 lbs.

New Forms

no. 384 058   72 point
3×A   4×a   4×1   1 fount about 20,45 lbs.

AaBbCcDdEeFfGg Hh Ii Jj Kk Ll Mm Nn Oo Pp Qq Rr Sss Tt UuVv Ww Xx Yy Zz $

277

Gillies Gothic bold

18 Point 7 A 24 a	*Swinburne's Poems and Novels*
24 Point 6 A 20 a	*Grand Evening Concert*
30 Point 5 A 16 a	*Kingston Orchestral*
36 Point 4 A 14 a	*Delicate charms*
48 Point 4 A 13 a	*Sven Hedin*
60 Point 3 A 10 a	*American*
72 Point 3 A 8 a	*Record*
84 Point 3 A 5 a	*Editor*
Announcement	*Gillies Gothic light will follow shortly*

Gillies Gothic combines perfectly with both classic and ultra modern types to create stunning new effects

THE S

20 EAST 761

CADILLAC MOTO

Music
Dramatics
Literature
Art

Aust

607 Fifth Avenue

Just seven drops

give you a velo-derma treatment.
Smoothed gently on the skin under
the usual daytime make-up, velo-
derma gives a fresh surface beauty
and does sound permanent improv-
ing at the same time. Try it-today!

ONLY AT

Saks Fifth Avenue

**ONLY FOR THIS WEEK, A NEW 6.00 BOTTLE
OF VELO-DERMA IS BEING FEATURED AT 2.00**

Certificate
Letter

Old-time Individuality Beauty and Character in Letter Paper

A BEAUTIFUL WHITE SHEET OF LAID BOND PAPER. THE IMPRESSION OF QUALITY AND DISTINCTION YOU WANT YOUR LETTERS TO CARRY CAN BE SECURED WITH CERTIFICATE LETTER, THE LAID COMPANION SHEET TO CERTIFICATE BOND. AN ADMIRABLE PAPER ALSO FOR ANNOUNCEMENTS AND ALL FINANCIAL ADVERTISING

Shurfine
Tea Bags

48 Count

45¢

El Wadora

GUARANTEED

QUALITY CIGAR

REGISTERED IN U.S. PATENT OFFICE

El Wadora

F. M. HOWELL & CO., ELMIRA, N. Y.

TITLE & DESIGN OWNED BY W. C. FRUTIGER & CO.

York Imperial

"SOME CIGAR"

Truly MILD

York Imperial

PANATELAS

VERY MILD

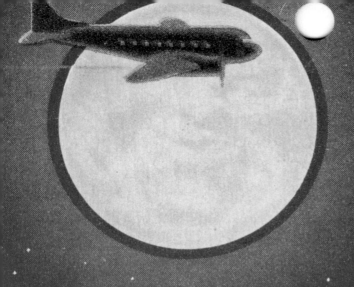

"FEEL LIKE A MILLION" **NR**

Nature's Remedy
REG. U.S. PAT. OFFICE

THE ALL VEGETABLE LAXATIVE

WEL

TUMS FOR THE TUMMY

FOR ACID INDIGESTION

Quinlan facial tissues

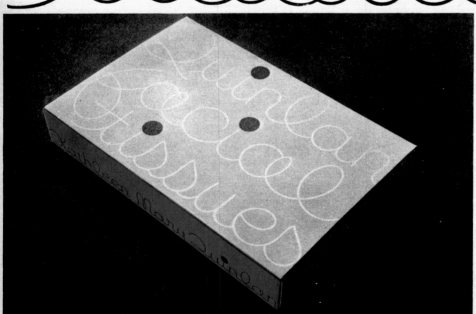

An adaptation of the single weight letter adapted from a Ronde form, applied to a tissue box design. Executed for Kathleen Mary Quinlan. Background Nile green, lettering in silver, dots black.

Photo: Arthur O'Neill.

Kathleen Mary Quinlan

Liberty Initials—Series C

Per Set, one of each, $7.50   Single Character 70c

A-1 A-2

I-1 I-2 J-1 J-2

P-1 P-2

R-1 R-2

Where two styles of initial are shown, order single character by initial and number as designated

Youth

Youth is not a time of life—it is a state of mind. It is not a matter of ripe cheeks, red lips and supple knees; it is a temper of the will, a quality of the imagination, a vigor of the emotions; it is a freshness of the deep springs of life.

Youth means a temperamental predominance of courage over timidity, of the appetite of adventure over love of ease. This often exists in a man of fifty more than in a boy of twenty.

Nobody grows old by merely living a number of years; people grow old only by deserting their ideals. Years wrinkle the skin, but to give up enthusiasm wrinkles the soul. Worry, doubt, self-distrust, fear and despair—these are the long, long years that bow the head and turn the growing spirit back to dust.

Whether seventy or sixteen, there is in every being's heart the love of wonder, the sweet amazement at the stars and the starlike things and thoughts, the undaunted challenge of events, the unfailing childlike appetite for what next, and the joy and the game of life.

You are as young as your faith, as old as your doubt; as young as your self-confidence, as old as your fear; as young as your hope, as old as your despair.

In the central place of your heart there is a wireless station; so long as it receives messages of beauty, hope, cheer, courage, grandeur and power from the earth, from men and from the Infinite, so long are you young.

When the wires are all down and all the central place of your heart is covered with the snows of pessimism and the ice of cynicism, then are you grown old indeed and may God have mercy on your soul.

ANONYMOUS

36 Point   4A 12a

Exceptionally Handsome Design Secured
Suitable for the Most Uptodate Concern

30 Point   5A 15a

The Highly Convincing Recommendation Useful
Seeking Employment — A Fine Reliable Branch

24 Point No. 2   6 A 18 a   18 Point   9 A 28 a

Politician Admits Errors Made   Productive Time Means Money
Furnishes Pleasing Explanation   Systematize Your Printing Plant
                                    Minimize Nonproductive Hours

24 Point No. 1   7 A 22 a   14 Point   10 A 40 a

Beautiful Product Highly Merited   This Most Particular Summer Resort
Assuring Positively Increase of Trade   Made Ample Provision in Entertaining
                                    Distinguished Guest for Ensuing Season

36 Point   3 A 10 a

The Spirit of Well Bred Refinement
Must Always Pervade Society Work

30 Point   3 A 12 a

Let Your Skill Have Full Play — Use But
Such Faces As Impart Qualities You Desired

24 Point No. 2   5 A 14 a   18 Point   8 A 22 a

General Information Obtained   Just As Proper Words in Speech
Through Local Departments   Must Be Used to Convey Right
                                    Idea So Must Type Be Chosen

24 Point No. 1   5 A 18 a   14 Point   9 A 35 a

Proudly We Display Our Correct   Full Authority Given the Capable Manager

42 Point   3 A 8 a

Pen Effect Close to Hand Lettered

36 Point   4 A 10 a   18 Point   6 A 19 a

Quality Gloss Embossed

Here Interesting Demands
Are Brought $1234567890

30 Point   4 A 12 a   12 Point   7 A 29 a

Many Ask Hugh Profit

Graceful Sloping Letter Most Usable
and Classier than Ordinary Script Design

All fonts contain *M Q u v ff ffi fl fl r s ss ß t ( )* special characters

---

CHESTER AUTO COMPANY

Have arranged for you to
Inspect during the week of October eleventh
their new 1930 Model

CHESTER TOURING CAR

which will be Exhibited in the
Gold Room of the Carlton Hotel
Lansing, Michigan

Please present this card
at the door

JOHN D. CHANDLER
President

---

30 Point   5 A 18 a

Beautiful Nifty Modish Graceful

24 Point   6 A 21 a

Unique Pretty Classy Results Charming Effect

18 Point   9 A 35 a   10 Point   10 A 48 a

Neat Tasteful Work Produced

Satisfactory Results Obtained on Work
Elegant Stylish Modern Pleasing Artful

293

Thorn Brothers and Maynard

PIANOS

Direct from Our Factory to Your Home
on Monthly Payments

East Upton, Ohio

Mrs. Agnes Drummond

invites the honor of your attendance at the

marriage of her daughter

Bertha May

to

Mr. James Oliver Barr

Saturday evening, December the twenty-eighth

Nineteen hundred and twenty-nine

at half-past eight o'clock

Castle Highway

Kenwood, New Jersey

Special Characters in upper line in all fonts
of French Plate Script

D L Th h to for ~ ( )
d r o'c ' '

Those below in all Wedding Plate fonts

D ~ h o'c r z ' '

Mr. George Edgar Read

Sleight of

hand?

Not exactly: We don't use mirrors or high silk hats. But we <u>do</u> work reproduction magic with hand-and-mind craftsmanship — Silk Screen Process at its best! What's your problem?...Counter Card, Poster, Salesman's Presentation, Short Run, Unusual Size or Printing Surface? Our craftsmen will solve it for you . . . efficiently . . . but economically!

Then let us regard as the aider of Art,
Each one who in printing doth bear the least part,
And whoe'er would oppress it must have a vile heart,
Then sing in the praise of good printing,
And sing in that noble Art's praise

FROM SONGS OF THE PRESS. LONDON 1845

Capon

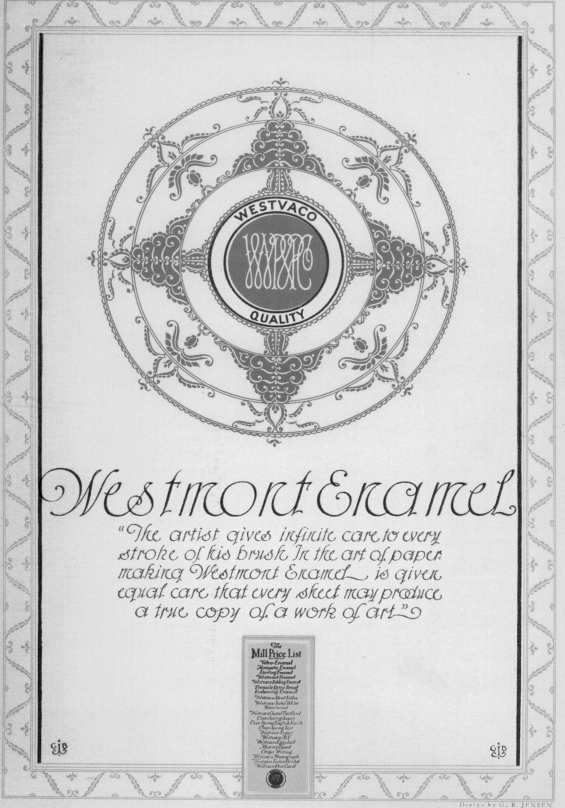

Westmont Enamel

"The artist gives infinite care to every stroke of his brush In the art of paper making Westmont Enamel is given equal care that every sheet may produce a true copy of a work of art"

Design by G. B. JENSEN

★

always right

STYLE · QUALITY · VALUE

THE JOHNSON *Shoe* leaves no doubt as to the quality of workmanship...every detail from the selection of the leather to the finished shoe is carefully watched to insure perfection. Johnson shoes are long on wear and short on up keep, for they are made of the most durable leather known. At $7.50 they are investment bargains. Come in and put on a pair; if you buy you must be satisfied or we will return your money.

Johnson Shoe Shops

EIGHT STORES IN THE LOOP

60 POINT

ABCDEFGHIJKL
MNOPQRSTUVW
XYZ& 1234567890$
abcdefghijklmnopqrstuvwxyz

72 Point   3 A 4 a

Great Cap Initial

60 Point   3 A 4 a   30 Point   5 A 17 a

Kept Out

Mandolin Exhibited
Produced Beautiful

54 Point   3 A 7 a   18 Point   9 A 28 a

Easiest Fight

Youngest Artist Rendered
Notes Charmingly Perfect

36 Point   3 A 9 a   14 Point   14 A 39 a

Blind Kid Joyful

Type is Much Cheaper Than Hand
Lettering is Today $1234567890

Kleaner Sanitowel

and Napkin Service

...er Towels for the Office

...Napkins for Restaurants

...Allowance for Used Goods

...y & Cashwell

...Street : Telephone Mars 237

Regal

Gowns

Millinery

Suits

Stevens Building
Ninth Floor

Announcement Supplement

Edwin Brockton & Carroll

a belated shipment of the very latest

Millinery

David H. Bornewall

Listern Company
39 Broadway   New York

and Saint Paul too late for display

in the Grand Spring Opening just closed

Owing to the delay large concessions
will be allowed on every imported design included
in this very extensive shipment

Pantagraph Script Series

60 Point   4 A   11 a

Mattson Business High School

48 Point   3 A   12 a

Handsomer Announcements Designed

36 Point   5 A   14 a

Distributes World Court

18 Point   10 A   26 a

Wedding Anniversaries Celebrated
Magnificent Receptions are Held

24 Point   7 A   20 a

Admission to Dances Magnificent

12 Point   13 A   36 a

Banks Solicited Funds for Operatic Artists
Personal Stationery Designings $1234567890

ABC
DEFGHIJKLMN
OPQuRSTUVW
XYZ

Gladiola

MEISLE
Star

at Roosevelt
Inaugural Concert

72 point Mondial Bold Condensed

14 point 4596 9 A 36 a	Useful Hints on Decorating and Brightening the Home this Spring
16 point 4597 8 A 28 a	Have Your Plymouth delivered with a Philco installed
18 point 4598 7 A 24 a	Artistic Printers Desire to Please their Customers
20 point 4599 6 A 22 a	It's thrifty to replace with a Delco Battery
24 point 4600 6 A 20 a	The Phrase Maker of the Potomac
30 point 4601 5 A 16 a	Electrical Standard of Living
42 point 4602 4 A 14 a	Ladies' Home Journal
54 point 4603 3 A 10 a	Greyhound Lines
72 point 4604 3 A 7 a	Advertisement

The Eagle Aircraft Corporation

Makers of fast Aircraft

EAGLE HOUSE · PALL MALL · W1

Ratio Roman Light Italic and Demi-Bold

Evening Gazette Reading

3694　18 point　10 A 20 a

Heatilator Fireplace

3695　20 point　8 A 15 a

Modern Printing

3696　24 point　5 A 10 a

Renart Studio

3697　30 point　4 A 8 a

Bolton's Poster Services

3698　36 point　3 A 6 a

Vaseline Hair Tonic

3699　54 point　3 A 5 a

United Air Lines

3700　60 point　3 A 4 a

306

"Comet" The Smash Hit
in Emerson Hats
for Springtime

$4 and $5. Other Qualities up to $7.50

Emerson Hats

EMERSON HAT COMPANY / NEW YORK

Ratio Roman Bold

A B C D E F G H I J K

L M N O P Q R S T U V W

X Y Z

a b c d e f g h i j k l

m n o p q r s t u v w x y z

ff fi fl & $ £

.,-:;!?'("" 1 2 3 4 5 6 7 8 9 0

THE PUBLICITY CLUB OF LONDON

Technical Study Section

Conducted by

ALFRED BASTIEN   W. H. BUTTLER   ROY HARDY

C. MAXWELL TREGURTHA   A. S. WILDMAN   E. J. TONER, Hon. Sec.

THE next meeting of the Technical Study Section on January 26th is of special interest and importance. The Bassett-Gray Studios were invited to address the members on this occasion, and this organisation has made such splendid arrangements, it was felt that a large number of members of the Club would desire to attend the meeting. The subject is

"The Techniques applicable to Advertising; how they are determined by the initial conception"

ANNOU

The first showing

Gowns and Frocks

will be put on exhibi

at four o'clock on

R.S.V.P. TO MAD

6, CARMELITE

Exhibition by Photographers in Advertising
12 point   4811   12 A 48 a

New York Life Insurance Company
14 point   4812   9 A 36 a

Bright and Pleasant Literature
16 point   4813   8 A 28 a

Combined with smart Display
18 point   4814   7 A 24 a

Delta Electric Company
24 point small face   4815   6 A 22 a

Universal Pictures
24 point large face   4816   6 A 20 a

Hotel Central
30 point   4817   5 A 16 a

Modern Designs
42 point   4818   4 A 14 a

Philadelphia
54 point   4819   3 A 10 a

November
66 point   4820   3 A 7 a

Ordinate
84 point   4821   3 A 5 a

In addition to the normal cutting a demi-bold face of the Discus is also available

No overhangs!

CING

latest designs of

...ning Wear which

...Salon des Arts

...y, August 27th.

E MADELEINE

ONDON, E.C.4

Grosvenor House
LONDON

Alice Beasley
24, Fleet Street, London E.C.4
Central 7208

*Modern
Photography*
for Commercial and
advertising purposes.
Illustrated
Catalogues and Leaflets

A B C D E F G G H I J K
L M N O P Q R S T
U V W X Y Z

a b c d e f g h i j k l m n o p q r s t u v w x y z

ff fi fl & $ £

. , - : ; ! ? ' ( ) " " 1 2 3 4 5 6 7 8 9 0 I V X

ALPHABETH OF THE DISCUS

It Pays T

The Quick Brown Fox Jumped Over The Lazy Hound Dogs
ACEGIKMNPRSU fb VWXYZ tlqj

FIGURE 94—Display Script

The Est

ABCDEFGHIJK
LMNOPQRSTUV
WXYZ
abcdefghijklmnopqr
stuvwxyz

FIGURE 93—Eccentric Script

ABCDE
FGHIJ
KLMN
OPQR
STUVW
XYZ &

abcdefghijklmn
opqrstuvwxyz

A B C D E F G H I

J K L M N O P Q

R S T U

V W X Y Z

FIGURE 96—Sign Painter's Script

1 2 3 4 5 6 7 8 9 0

go lazy fat vixen &

be shrewd jump quick

FIGURE 96 (Continued)—Sign Painter's Script

Radial  *Italic.*

40a 8A $8 85   GREAT PRIMER RADIAL ITALIC   20a 4A $4 50

Bethany, Mo., Dec. 20, 1884.

Barnhart Bros. & Spindler,

    Gentlemen:--After eighteen months use of a Bab-cock Country Press, I can say I am more than satisfied with it in every respect.   I believe it to be the best press made for the money, or sold as a Country Press.

         Yours Respectfully,

               F. H. Ramer.

Artistic   *Script.*

PATENT APPLIED FOR.

Battle Creek, Mich., Nov. 14, 1884.

Barnhart Bros. & Spindler,

    Gentlemen:--The longer we run the Babcock Press purchased of you, the better we like it.   It works noiselessly; the Tapeless Delivery and Air Springs work to perfection.   Every one admires the ease with which it runs, as also the many Convenient Improvements, such as the Eccentric Throw-off for throwing the Ink Rollers off the forms, the handy Lock-up, Cover to Air Springs, etc.   The Press does more than you claim for it.

         Very Truly Yours,

               M. E. Brown.

DBL. PICA ARTISTIC SCRIPT.
   20a 7A $7 00

This Script is cut with less slope than any others of same character: the letters overhang comparatively little, consequently will prove more durable.

Office Barnhart Bros. & Spindler,

M'f'rs Celebrated Superior Copper=Mixed Type

115=117 Fifth Avenue.   Chicago, February, 1885.

Dear Sir: Our Superior Copper=Mixed Type has fairly

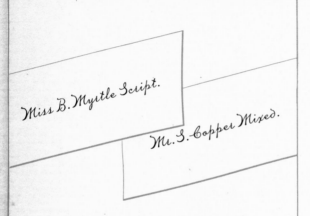

Miss B. Myrtle Script.

Mr. S. Copper Mixed.

Married
Miss Beautiful Myrtle Script,
to
Mr. Superior Copper Mixed,
Thursday Afternoon, October twenty third,
eighteen hundred and eighty four,
Chicago, Illinois.

no successful rival in market.   We shall continue to main=
tain the high standard of excellence which it has always
enjoyed, relying for support upon the class of customers who
prefer and are willing to pay fair prices for the best material.
Soliciting your further orders, we remain

Yours Respectfully,

Barnhart Bros. & Spindler.

MYRTLE SCRIPT.

Double Pica,	6oa 10A	$11 25
" "	3oa 5A	6 00
Great Primer,	8oa 12A	9 00
" "	4oa 6A	5 00

Spinner Script.

PATENTED.

Job Fonts, 15A, 75a, $8.00.   PICA SPINNER SCRIPT.   Card Fonts, 6A, 25a, $3.25.

We take pleasure in introducing to our Friends and Patrons the "Pica Spinner Script." The popularity of this Face has been greatly stimulated by the addition of this, the minimum size of the Series. Printers will notice that its Compactness, Legibility and Freedom from Kerned Letters (enabling it to be set solid), makes it available in places where many other styles of Type would be impracticable. By the

American System of
Interchangeable Type Bodies

The Artistic Printer will be able to work it to advantage with the other sizes, producing effects that will be pleasing and fulfilling the requirements of good taste. The handsome appearance of the Pica Spinner Script speaks more decidedly than any words, but we must state that in addition to its Great Beauty it possesses Wearing Qualities no less desirable and important.   1 2 3 4 5 6 7 8 9 0 $ & ℔ ¢ ℔

Job Fonts, 12A, 60a, $10.00.   GREAT PRIMER SPINNER SCRIPT.   Card Fonts, 6A, 16a, $4.35.

We offer for the approval of the Craft this the Great Primer Size of our Spinner Script; its style is striking and suggestive of uncommon durability. By the absence of kerned letters, the hair lines are so well protected that they will stand as strong a pressure as any portion of the letter. It combines qualities Printers have long felt the need of in scripts, namely: Novelty, Gracefulness, Legibility and freedom from too much ornamentation, making it one of the most useful Scripts that has yet been designed. Used in connection with the other sizes in Circulars, Letter Heads, etc., very pleasing results may be attained.

1 2 3 4 5 6 7 8 9 0 $ & ℔ ¢ ℔

SWEDISH, GERMAN AND SPANISH ACCENTS ARE CAST WITH ALL SIZES OF THIS SERIES AND ARE FURNISHED UPON APPLICATION.

NONPAREIL TELESCOPIC GOTHIC ITALIC.

PRICE OF SERIES COMPLETE, $4.75.

32A   NONPAREIL TELESCOPIC GOTHIC ITALIC, NO. 1. $1.00.

THE BOOK IS COMPLETED, AND CLOSED LIKE THE DAY, AND THE
HAND THAT HAS WRITTEN IT LAYS IT AWAY, DIM GROW ITS FANCIES, FORGOTTEN THEY LIE
LIKE COALS IN THE ASHES THEY DARKEN AND DIE 234

32A   NONPAREIL TELESCOPIC GOTHIC ITALIC, NO. 2. $1.05.

SONG SINKS INTO SILENCE, THE STORY IS TOLD, THE WINDOWS
DARKENED, THE HEARTH-STONE IS COLD, DARKER AND DARKER THE BLACK SHADOWS
FALL SLEEP AND OBLIVION REIGN OVER ALL 567

32A   NONPAREIL TELESCOPIC GOTHIC ITALIC, NO. 3. $1.20.

SOLEMNLY, MOURNFULLY, DEALING ITS DOLE, THE CURFEW
BELL IS BEGINNING TO TOLL, COVER THE EMBERS, PUT OUT THE LIGHT
TOIL COMES WITH THE MORNING, AND REST WITH THE NIGHT 234

32A   NONPAREIL TELESCOPIC GOTHIC ITALIC, NO. 4. $1.50.

DARK GROW THE WINDOWS AND QUENCHED
IS THE FIRE, SOUND FADES INTO SILENCE, ALL FOOTSTEPS
RETIRE, THERE IS NO VOICE IN THE CHAMBERS 23

ONE IS PAINED TO FIND THAT THE MOST EXCLUSIVE FOLKS HAVE FREQUENTLY PASSED
THEIR EARLY DAYS IN SELLING TAPE OR WEST INDIA GOODS IN HOMŒOPATHIC QUANTITIES. NOW THIS IS NOT AN
IMMORAL THING IN ITSELF, BUT IT IS CERTAINLY VERY ILLOGICAL OF THESE PEOPLE TO BE SO INTOLERANT OF THOSE LESS
FORTUNATE ONES WHO HAVE NOT YET DISPOSED OF THEIR STOCK
THICK SETTLED HAMLETS CLUSTER ROUND THE SILVERY LAKES AND STREAMS OF LIGHT WHILE THICKLY STUDDED STARS ABOVE DWELL IN THE AZURE SKIES AT NIGHT

MARDER, LUSE & CO., TYPE FOUNDERS, CHICAGO.

MARDER, LUSE & CO. TYPE FOUNDERS.

AMERICAN SYSTEM OF INTERCHANGEABLE TYPE BODIES. THE ONLY TRUE STANDARD.

AMERICAN SYSTEM OF INTERCHANGEABLE TYPE BODIES.

PATENT APPLIED FOR.

Card Fonts, 6A, 16a, $3.75 — GREAT PRIMER. — Job Fonts, 10A, 75a, $10.75

The Farmers & Drovers National Bank, of Bloomington, Illinois

Capital, $1,600,000.   Surplus, $755,000

Transact a General Banking business   Accounts of Individuals, Corporations and

Banks received.   Collections throughout the United States

National State and County Bonds on hand.   Commission Orders filled

Exchange drawn on England, Scotland, Ireland

Card Fonts, 4A, 12a, $4.50 — DOUBLE PICA. — Job Fonts, 8A, 50a, $12.55

Buckingham, Struthers, Lyons & Co.

Invite inspection of their Large and Varied stock of Art Goods

Unequalled Assortment of Fine and Curious Pieces

Complete in Every Department

Modern and Antique Cabinet Work, Marbles, Bronzes, Etc.

158 and 160 Yonge Street, San Francisco

Card Fonts, 3A, 8a, $4.75 — DOUBLE COLUMBIAN. — Job Fonts, 5A, 25a, $10.80

(Incorporated 1835.)

Erie & Ontario Fire and Marine Insurance Co

Accumulated Capital, $800,000.

Hazardous Risks taken at Lowest Premiums

Ladies Hand Script, No. 2.

SPECIMENS FROM FARMER, LITTLE & CO., TYPE FOUNDERS.

NEW YORK—63 & 65 Beekman St.
And 62 & 64 Gold Street.

CHICAGO—154 Monroe Street,
Chas. B. Ross, Manager.

PATENT PENDING.

36 a 9 A—Price per Font, $8 00   THREE LINE NONPAREIL STATIONER SCRIPT—18 POINT.   LOWER CASE, $5 00

The Firm has much pleasure in returning their Thanks to

The American Printing Trade

For the Appreciation with which they have received the Stationer Script

And now Complete the Series with this New Size

Which they present to the Trade in Compliance with the Demand

Made for its Production

20 a 6 A—Price per Font, $8 00   TWO LINE PICA STATIONER SCRIPT—24 POINT.   LOWER CASE, $5 00

We Request the Attention of the Printing Trade to

This Elegant New Script Face

Designed Expressly for the Printing of Wedding and Visiting

Cards, Invitation Notes, etc.,

The Name Stationer Script will be appropriate

15 a 5 A—Price per Font, $9 50   THREE LINE PICA STATIONER SCRIPT—36 POINT.   LOWER CASE, $5 75

The Three Sizes in Combination are

Very Handsome in Appearance

Attractive and Useful in Character it will be

A General Favorite

FARMER, LITTLE & CO., TYPE FOUNDERS, CHICAGO.

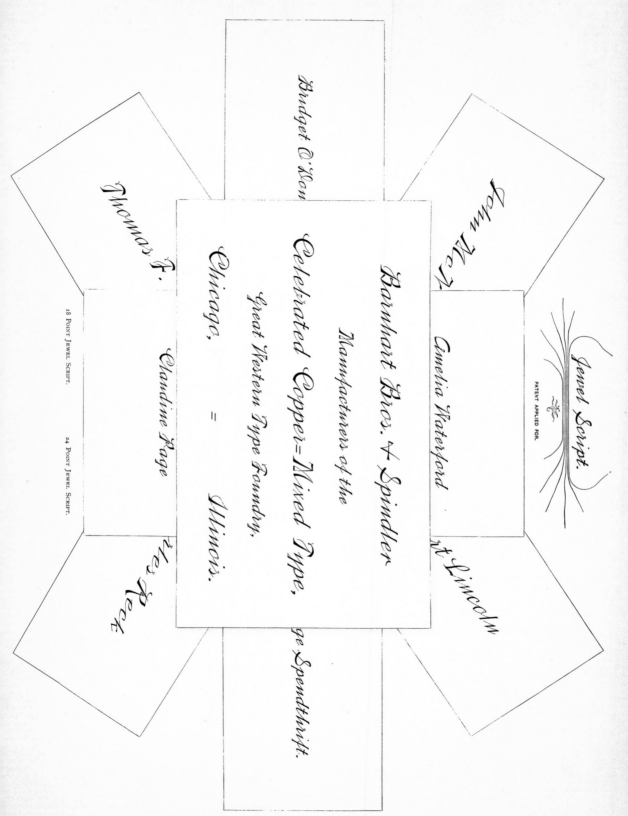

319

4A, 18a.   30 POINT HOYT SCRIPT. $8.85
                                            Card Fonts, 3A, 8a, 4.75

The following is what the Iowa Press Association made of Horace Greeley's note declining the invitation to meet with them the following June:

"I have wondered all along whether any squint had denied the scandal of the President meeting June in the woods on Saturday. I have hominy, carrots, and R. R. ties more than I can mow with eight steam. If eels are blighted, dig them early. Any insinuation that brick coins are dangerous to hams gives me the horrors."

Yours Truly,

Horace Greeley.

Keystone Pen Writer

KEYSTONE TYPE FOUNDRY.

PATENTED MAY 7, 1889.

INVENTORS OF NICKEL ALLOY TYPE METAL.

NINE-POINT.   12 A. 32 a. $3.45   32 a. $2.00

Its health-restoring qualities are becoming celebrated the world over

Little by little they go through a course of important reading

Do not try to make up the deficiency in price by the deficiency in workmanship; rather incur
loss than furnish inferior work of any kind

The severe gale which visited the coast during March. $1234567890

TWELVE-POINT.   12 A. 32 a. $4.64   32 a. $2.90

Do not marry until you are able to support a wife

Fun for fun.   Business for business.

If any one speak evil of you, let your life be so that none will believe it

Push is the word for a world full of work as this is

Receipts $1,234,567,890

EIGHTEEN-POINT.   8 A. 20 a. $5.65   20 a. $3.25

An Account of my Experience

It is not well for one to have too many intimate friends

No Indication of being Discouraged

$1234567890

TWENTY-FOUR-POINT.   6 A. 14 a. $5.90   14 a. $3.40

Promoting Happiness

Several Celebrated Characters of this Age

Aid Given in the Right Direction

$1234567890

CAST FROM OUR NICKEL ALLOY TYPE METAL—SUPERIOR TO ALL OTHERS.

MATHER MANUFACTURING CO.
PROPRIETORS.

✠

734 TO 740 SANSOM STREET,
PHILADELPHIA.

PATENT APPLIED FOR.

Mr. and Mrs. V. T. Montague,

At Home
Friday, October 13th & 19th
3465 North Park Lane.

Mr. and Mrs. Rochester
request your presence
at the marriage of their daughter
Georgiana
to
Vincent Favin Montague,
Wednesday evening, October eighth,
Eighteen hundred and ninety-three
at eight o'clock.

Mr. & Burlington,
Los Angeles,
California.

1657 Belthino Avenue.

14 Point :—
  9 A 30 a $5 50

18 Point :—
  9 A 25 a $6 40

24 Point :—
  7 A 20 a $8 00

Manufactured by BARNHART BROS. & SPINDLER, Chicago, Ill.

SHEPARD SCRIPT SERIES.

Originated by THE CRESCENT TYPE FOUNDRY, 349 & 351 Dearborn Street, Chicago.

4A. 8a.   48 POINT SHEPARD SCRIPT $8.00

—All Careful Employers—

Steel Plate and Letter Press Printers

Efforts of Atlanta People

5A. 12a.   36 POINT SHEPARD SCRIPT $6.75

Some Departures in Type Founding

Many Beautiful Original Designs Shown Here

Glad Holiday Festivities Coming

6A. 18a.   24 POINT SHEPARD SCRIPT $5.25

May We Still Remember to Celebrate Christmas

Resort to Every Method to Introduce the Standard Lining System

Meritorious Efforts Should be Appreciated

8A. 18a.   18 POINT SHEPARD SCRIPT $3.75

The Attention of Printers and the Trade is Called to This New Face

It Being the First Script Ever Made on the Standard Line, Point System and Unit Set

Is Neat and Appropriate for All Classes of Fine Work

KEPT IN STOCK AND FOR SALE BY THE FOLLOWING FIRMS:

INLAND TYPE FOUNDRY, St. Louis, Mo.
KEYSTONE TYPE FOUNDRY, Philadelphia.
PACIFIC STATES TYPE FOUNDRY, San Francisco.

GOLDING & CO., Boston, New York, Chicago.
CONNER, FENDLER & CO., New York.
DOMINION PRINTERS SUPPLY CO., Toronto, Can.

Clark Script

ORIGINATED BY BOSTON TYPE FOUNDRY, BOSTON, MASS.

24 POINT   7 A 20 a $5 00

Afternoon Excursion to Marblehead and Immediate Neighborhood

Boats Leaving Hourly 75cts Round Trip.

Splendid Accommodations and Finest Refreshments

Immediate action necessary on the part of excursionists for guarantee of upper deck seats. Purchasers of tickets should remember this fact thereby avoiding disappointment. Exceptional advantages offered to Picnic, Family and Society parties by management of this popular steamship company.   Opening of season by trips to Nantasket, Downer Landing and Gloucester at half usual prices.

Cleveland Script

PATENTED

ORIGINATED BY CLEVELAND TYPE FOUNDRY, CLEVELAND, O.

24 POINT   8 A 32 a $8 50   4 A 16 a $4 50

Cleveland Harbor Lake Erie September 27th 1894

Fourteen Moonlight Masqueraders Depart

We here present for your approval the unique scheme of every Loyal Sir Knight contributing to the Relief Fund his ratio of amount annually appropriated for the handsomest mascot in the Conclave.

Believing that you will agree with us that the proposition is most worthy and trusting that you

Circular Script

PATENTED

ORIGINATED BY MACKELLAR, SMITHS & JORDAN FOUNDRY, PHILADELPHIA

18 POINT — 10 A 50 a $12 20

Hardscrabble, Oct. 30, 1885.

Messrs. Rubhard & Co

I am troubled with a feeling of Drowsiness, Weakness of the Back, with general Indisposition to Labour. The symptoms commence on Monday morning and last till Saturday evening. If you can help me you will oblige

Gregory Lackthrift

12 POINT — 10 A 50 a $7 00

Busy Town, Nov. 2, 1885.

Gregory Lackthrift, Esq.

Having carefully studied the symptoms of your case, we have forwarded to your address a package of Elbow Grease, which, if diligently applied, from 7 a. m. to 6 p. m., daily, will relieve your troubles. To prevent a relapse, Industrious Habits must be cultivated.

Yours respectfully,

Rubhard & Co

24 POINT — 10 A 50 a $18 65

Eureka, March 31, 1896.

To improve the national morals we decide to erect, in every county of the United States, a Whipping=post and Ducking=stool, for the punishment of knavish and quarrelsome persons

36 POINT   3 A 4 A 12 a $11 90

Latest Artistic Fancy

Just the style of Type needed for printing Diplomas or Certificates

24 POINT   3 A 5 A 20 a $8 40

Quaintly Harmonizing Letters

Here is shown a production of letter able to resist the every-day wear of a printing office

18 POINT   3 A 5 A 25 a $6 30

Eagerness for Fanciful Conceits

Unceasing demands are made by Printers for Styles of Type adapted expressly for Fine Job Work. This Script is well adapted for Cards, Circulars, Bill Headings, etc.

ABIFKMNOPRTVWXYZ

12 POINT   10 A 50 a $5 20

Nineteenth Century Advantages and Facilities

At the present day, with the help of the Steam-engine, Printing-press, Telegraph, and other modern labor and time saving appliances, many large and profitable Business Enterprises can be inaugurated and perpetuated with a facility that would have appeared incredible to our ancestors; and the judicious use of Type and Ink is probably the most valuable auxiliary available in this age of progress

Cursive Script

ORIGINATED BY DICKINSON TYPE FOUNDERY, BOSTON, MASS.

18 POINT   10 A 40 a $6 00   40 a $3 25

Boston, Mass., January, 1894.

To Artistic Printers:

This Cursive Script is an imitation of a fashion of writing which was popular in France during the Sixteenth Century. Nicholas Granjon, a French Engraver, cut the first punches at Lyons during the year 1556. The King gave him exclusive privilege to manufacture the Civilitie for ten years.

The Cursive was then known as Civilitie, and was so called from the title of a book of precepts, which was frequently reprinted in these types with intent to teach French children to read the fashionable handwriting of the day.

Admirers of eccentric characters will find in the Cursive pleasing varieties of Mediaeval forms in both the Capitals and Lower Case, models of shapes designed by the masters of early type printing.

They have been displaced by reason of changes in taste but they are being restored to favor, and will gratify those who delight in the quaintness and strength of the old-time master printers

Dickinson Type Foundery

Old Style Script

PATENTED

ORIGINATED BY CENTRAL TYPE FOUNDRY, ST. LOUIS, MO.

30 POINT   6 A 18 a $9 00

Specimens of Ancient Carving
Collect 247 Designs
While upon the time-stained pages of our
history are blazoned deeds of valor by men

24 POINT   6 A 20 a $8 00

Mutual Reserve Fund Life Insurance
Reliable Agents Wanted $187
Doubtless, considerable secrecy accompanied all of the
operations of the first printers, and was maintained

18 POINT   8 A 24 a $6 00

Renowned Literary Experts Explaining Methods
Received Friday, January 26th, 1894
There is a statement current that Schoeffer was the first type
founder, but that is probably inaccurate, as the man who inven-

12 POINT   10 A 32 a $5 00

Rambles with Feminine Beauties Cause Matrimonial Thoughts of Love
The Morning Bulletin $250 and Evening Regulator
While upon the time-stained pages of history are blazoned deeds of valor by men who gloried in
bloodshed and carnage, should we not rather cherish the memory of those who, silently and without
ostentation, have been a blessing to mankind and an honor to their country. Such is the history of

24 POINT   6 A 22 a $7.00

Doolittle & Loafer Manufacturing Company
925 Chestnut Park, Kentucky
    The evils of which we complain are those
most common in the larger cities where the com=
petition for vacancies by boys in all branches of
business is most severe; and where, as a rule,
the time ordinarily required for the acquisition
of an education is notably shortened in order
that the labor of the boy may be made available
A A M S W W & Co Ch Co tt

16 POINT   10 A 44 a $6.00

From the Office of U. R. A. Hustler & Co., Printers
307 Business Street, Waltham, Mass.

    There is nothing that adds more to the neatness and attrac-
tiveness of job work or composition of any kind, outside of good
presswork, than correct and proper spacing and justification.   I
do not mean by this the setting apart at regular intervals in a
line each individual word, as generally understood among a large
majority of printers, but the more comprehensive system of equal
balance on all sides of words, lines, letters, and so on.   I fear
book spacing is too often understood to mean each word just so
far from its next fellow, without regard to making the next line
conform to the one above in thin or thick spacing.   Too often
A A M M S S W W & Co Ch Co th

German, French and Spanish Accents are made for the Manuscript Series.   Not sent unless especially ordered.

Parisian Series

PATENTED

18 POINT   16A 50a $6 00   8A 16a $3 00

From Gallery of Learned Men in Typography.

Conrad Zeltner, in his Gallery of Learned Men who have excelled in the honorable art of typography, printed at Nuremburg in 1716, said that it was the custom, in all the early printing offices to employ a man whose duty it was to read illegible copy aloud to compositors who set the types by dictation, never seeing the copy. He said that the reader could read to three or four compositors from as many different copies.

24 POINT   10A 40a $7 00   5A 12a $3 50

Pierre Moreau, of Paris, in the year 1640, designed a new form of writing types with bold and eccentric capitals, but with straight and unconnected lower case letters, not unlike those now known as Secretary, but of much more ungraceful shape. He dedicated the type to Louis 13th, who rewarded him with the title of King's Printer. Moreau used this face of type as the text letter of many books.

12 POINT   16A 50a $4 90

Benj. Franklin to William Strahan, Aug. 19, 1784.

I remember once your observing to me in the House of Commons that no two journeymen printers within your knowledge, had met with such success as ourselves. You were then at the head of your profession, and soon afterward became a Member of Parliament. I was agent for a few provinces, but now I act for them all. But we have risen by different modes. I as a Republican Printer, liked a form well planed down. You as a Monarchist, chose to work on crown paper and found it profitable, whilst I worked upon foolscap, with no less advantage.

Mr. & Mrs. Hornbrook.

SKINNER SCRIPT
18 POINT 7 A 22a $4 00

Admit Bearer

Boston Common, July 4th

Park Street Gate

MAGNOLIA SCRIPT
24 POINT 7 A 20a $7 00

Spring Goods

*Having completed extensive alterations in
our large Emporium, the undersigned would call
attention to an extensive line of*

Millinery Trimmings

*which have arrived from London and Paris,
and are the finest in this city.*

Madame Lecomte.

QUINCY SCRIPT
24 POINT 5 A 16a $4 25
36   4 A 9a 5 00
48   3 A 6a 6 00

Katie M. Irish.

Boston

James Woods & Co.

Chicago

AUTOGRAPH SCRIPT
24 POINT 7 A 20a $8 00

Miss Teresa Madigan.

Mr. William H. Leavey.

Master Eben Mansfield.

SKINNER SCRIPT
12 POINT 10 A 28a $3 30

Novelty Script

ORIGINATED BY CENTRAL TYPE FOUNDRY, ST. LOUIS, MO.

72 POINT   3A 4a $16 00

Charts 25 Antler

Hand Lattice

80 POINT   3A 5a $11 05

Cordial 76 Banged

Roman Grave

332

48 POINT 3A 6a $9 00

Breast Pin 5 Lake Trout

Dead Squirrels

36 POINT 4A 8a $7 25

Daily Records 14 Glorious Time

Vigilant and Valkyric

24 POINT 5A 16a $4 00

Townships and $975 Precincts

King's Private Lodge

18 POINT 5A 12a $5 25

Beautiful $5 Scotland

Pure Grape Juice

TOTAL PAYMENTS TO POLICY-HOLDERS SIN
HELD FOR THE

The Mauh

64-66-68 & 70 BROADWAY.

M. L. BUH

8625 162nd S

Jamaica,

Phone: Jamaica 2878

ORGANIZATION PLUS THE AMOUNT NOW
BENEFIT $117,721,022.

attau Life

ORGANIZED 1850

surance Company

OF NEW YORK

R

Blum & Rubenoff, WOOLENS

98-100 FIFTH AVE.,

New York

H. Krieger Son & Co. MEN'S Fine Neckwear

751 BROADWAY

NEW YORK

Schmidt's Café

FRED. P. SCHMIDT PROP.

400 MYRTLE AVE.

BOROUGH OF Brooklyn, N.Y.

TELEPHONE 2477 PROSPECT

Charles Roland

BAKERY

MAIN STREET.

FORT LEE, N. J.

ROYAL HUDSON CO.

OBESITY OIL

American Office,
Hudson Building,
32 Broadway.

New York

H. W. CLARK

MAKER OF

PORTRAITS

ENLARGING OF ALL KINDS.   WATER COLORS.   PASTELS & CRAYONS.

Cumberland, Md. _____ 19

Specimens of Letterheads and Scripts

(TO ORDER)

While our chief work consists in designing unique Cuts, we also have thousands of Stock Cuts on hand.

Specimens of Various Styles of Script

(TO ORDER)

We can design the most delicate script, for we employ competent men in this line. Let us submit sketches for approval. Positively no sketches made on speculation.

PHONE 3943 SPRING

New York
Coat Front & Pad Company.
INCORPORATED
113 - 115 - 117 Spring St.

Manuel Caragol.
Departamento de Tejidos.
Representado por
Sarcada & Co
Habana, Cuba
82 Beaver St.
New York.

ESTABLISHED 1874

John Fennell,
Manufacturer of
Awnings, Flags & Shades, Flag poles repaired & Painted,
Boiler & Pipe Coverings, Canvas articles of
every Description.
1284 Third Ave.,
NEAR 74th ST
New York.

L. Germansky,
Importer and Jobber of
Popular Merchandise
552 - 554 Fifth Ave.,
Brooklyn, N. Y.

The *Smith* Dry Goods Co.
DRY GOODS CLOAKS AND CARPETS

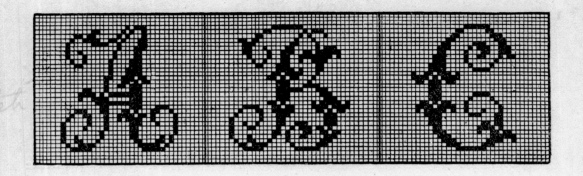

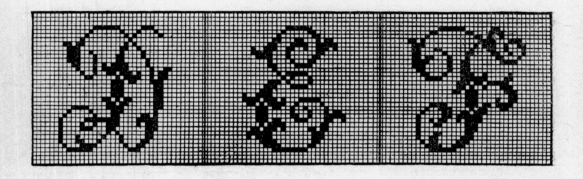

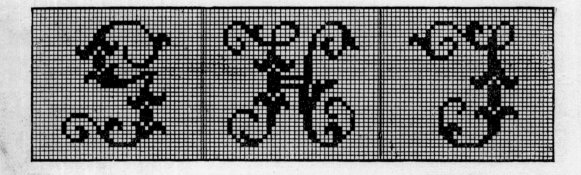

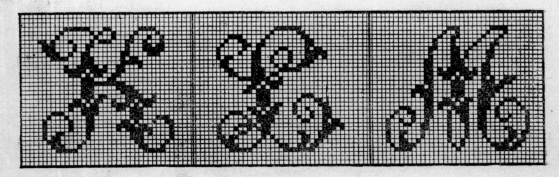

340

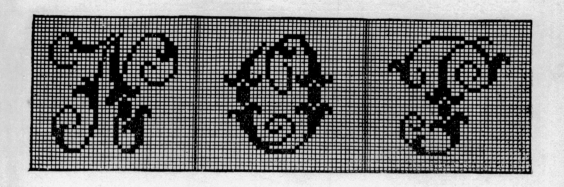

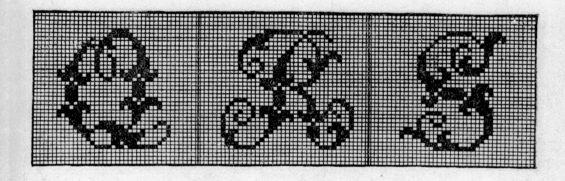

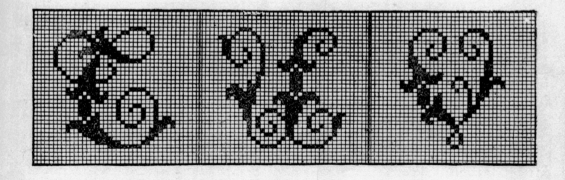

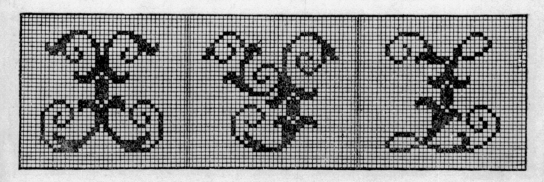

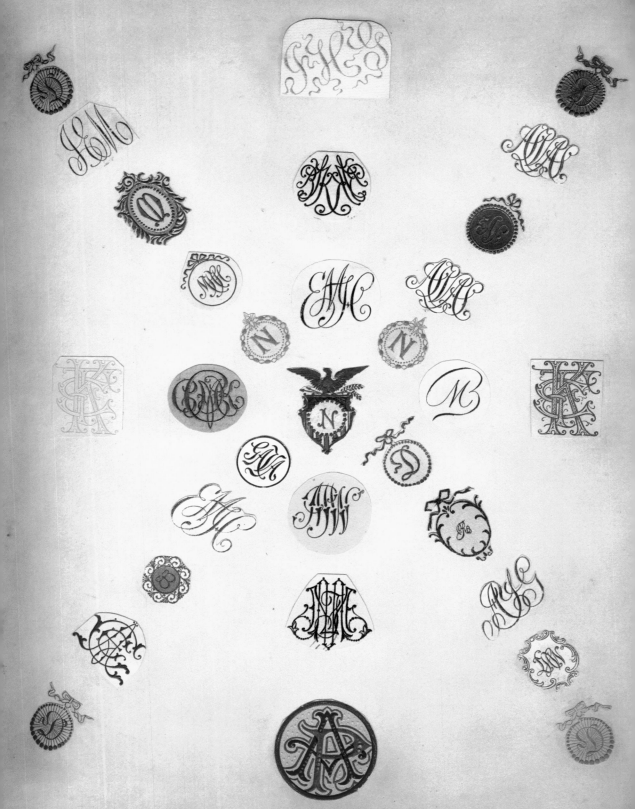

GRAND HOTEL,
MACKINAC ISLAND.
HENRY WEAVER.

Hotel Chelsea
Atlantic City, N.J.

GRAND UNION.
SARATOGA SPRINGS.

PAUL SMITH'S
IN THE ADIRONDACKS
PAUL SMITH'S, N.Y.

MANHATTAN BEACH HOTEL
T. F. SILLECK.
MANHATTAN BEACH, N.Y.

The Utowana.
BLUE MOUNTAIN LAKE,
HAMILTON CO. N.Y.
J. B. WHITE, SUPERINTENDENT.

Hite Arms Hotel,
BRAEMAR.

The Edgerton,
Delhi, N.Y.
M. E. Arbuckle, Prop.

HOTEL GRAY & D'ALBION
CANNES

The Windsor
MONTREAL.

WHITE HART HOTEL
LINCOLN

THE SHOREHAM
JOHN T. DEVINE.
WASHINGTON, D.C.

THE LAKE HOUSE
Lake George, N.Y.

THE WESTMINSTER
BOSTON, MASSACHUSETTS.
HARRY L. BROWN, MANAGER.

The Windsor
MONTREAL.

Hotel Luray
DIRECTLY ON THE BEACH
Atlantic City, N.J.

The Windsor
MONTREAL.

346

WHO THE IS THIS FROM?

Gilbert & Bacon
WE CHAIN THE SUN TO SERVE US
PHOTOGRAPHIC STUDIO
1030 CHESTNUT ST PHILADELPHIA

FROM ONE TO ANOTHER

LAW OFFICES OF
HISCOCK, DOHENY, WILLIAMS & COWIE
SYRACUSE, N.Y.

RENSSELAER COUNTY COURT,
HENRY T. NASON,
COUNTY JUDGE.

JOHN E. POUND,
COUNSELLOR AT LAW,
LOCKPORT, N.Y.

LAW OFFICES
STEDMAN & STEDMAN,
NO. 445 BROADWAY,
ALBANY, N.Y.
GEORGE W. STEDMAN. CHARLES S. STEDMAN

Royal Engraving Co
17 S. NINTH ST.,
Philadelphia, Pa.

J. NEWTON FIERO,
51 State Street,
Albany, N.Y.

Crouse & Perkins,
Counsellors at Law,
Jersey City, N.J.

William M. Butler,
COUNSELLOR AT LAW,
434-438 TREMONT BUILDING,
BOSTON.

RETURN AFTER 5 DAYS
ALBANY, N.Y.
QUAYLE & SON

Griffin and Young,
Attorneys and Counselors at Law,
White Plains, N.Y.

WEDDING INVITATIONS VISITING CARDS &C.
O. M. PADDOCK
ENGRAVER & PRINTER
PUBLIC SQUARE
WATERTOWN, NEW YORK.

NATIONAL COMMERCIAL BANK
ALBANY, N.Y.

NASH ROCKWOOD,
ATTORNEY AT LAW,
378 BROADWAY,
SARATOGA SPRINGS, N.Y.

EDITORIAL ROOMS
The Troy Times.
Charles S. Francis.

Milo J. White,
Counselor at Law,
Mount Vernon, N.Y.
POST OFFICE BUILDING,
16 EAST FIRST STREET.

THE WAIST HOUSE

Geo. A. Sullivan.

THE ALBANY TRUST CO.
ALBANY, N.Y.

LAW OFFICE,
EDWIN VAN WORMER,
TWEDDLE BUILDING,
ALBANY, N.Y.

Henry Schachte,
Insurance, Real Estate,
Stocks & Bonds.
Charleston, S.C.

ERWIN L. HOCKRIDGE,
ATTORNEY AND COUNSELLOR,
MANN BUILDING, UTICA, N.Y.

347

238–39. Custom-painted window sign for Martin's store in New York, date unknown.

240–41. Novelty scripts from *New Letters and Lettering* by Paul Carlyle and Guy Oring, 1938.

242–47. Pages from an instruction guide on how to create brush lettering for retail businesses, 1935.

248–49. Specimen sheet for Mandate, a script used for informal advertising display, *c.* 1940.

250–51. Specimen sheet for Boulevard, a Berthold Foundry face distributed by Amsterdam Continental Types, New York, 1938.

252–53. Specimen sheet for Caprice, a Berthold Foundry face distributed by Amsterdam Continental Types, New York, 1938.

254–55. Specimen sheet for Reiner Black, designed by Imre Reiner, a Berthold Foundry face distributed by Amsterdam Continental Types, New York, 1938.

256–59. Various scripts from *New Letters and Lettering* by Paul Carlyle and Guy Oring, 1938.

260–63. Specimen sheets for the New Civilité Type Series, a French-inspired face, from American Type Founders Co., 1933.

264–65. Specimen sheet for Trafton Script designed by Howard Trafton, distributed by American Type Founders Co., 1933.

266–67. Specimen sheet for Raleigh Initials designed by Willard Sniffin, distributed by American Type Founders Co., 1929.

268–69. Specimen sheet for Raleigh Cursive designed by Willard Sniffin, distributed by American Type Founders Co., 1929.

270–71. Specimen pages for Lining Plate Script No. 2 from *Book of Type Specimens*, Barnhart Bros. & Spindler's Type Founders, Chicago, 1910.

272–73. Specimen pages for Lining Grace Script from *Book of Type Specimens*, Barnhart Bros. & Spindler's Type Founders, Chicago, 1910.

274–75. Specimen sheet for Ludlow Mandate, distributed by the Ludlow Typograph Co., Chicago, 1938.

276. Specimen sheet for Brush Script from *Book of American Types*, American Type Founders, 1934.

277. Specimen sheet for Signal Medium, a German script, from *Book of American Types*, American Type Founders, 1934.

278–79. Specimen sheet for Gillies Gothic Bold from American Type Founders, 1934.

280. Lightline script used for advertisement for laid bond paper, *c.* 1933.

281. Silkscreen sale poster with logo for Shurfine stores, *c.* 1950s.

282–87. Various cigar-box labels using custom and bastardized script lettering, 1900–50.

288. Brand name for Nature's Remedy laxative, with extra-wide swash, 1930s.

289. Advertisement and package design for Quinlan Facial Tissues that uses a variant of Ronde Script, 1928.

290–91. Specimen sheet for Liberty Initials Series C from American Type Founders, 1934.

292–95. Specimen sheets for French Plate Script and Stationers Semiscript from

American Type Founders, 1934.

296–97. Shadow version of script on an advertisement for a silkscreen printer, 1934.

298–99. Pages from Westvaco Inspirations *Guide for Printers and Designers* (designed by Capon, left; Gustav Jensen, right), 1924.

300–1. Specimen sheet for Mayfair from American Type Founders, 1934.

302. Specimen sheet for Advertisers Upright Script from American Type Founders, 1934.

303. Specimen sheet for Pantagraph Script Series from American Type Founders, 1934.

304–5. Specimen sheet for Gladiola from American Type Founders, 1937.

306–7. Specimen sheet for Ratio from American Type Founders, 1930.

308–9. Specimen sheet for Discus from American Type Founders, 1930.

310–11. Specimen page for Display Script and Eccentric Script from *Modern Sign Painting* by Edward J. Duvall, 1952.

312–13. Specimen pages for Sign Painter's Script from *Modern Sign Painting* by Edward J. Duvall, 1952.

314–15. Specimen page for Radial Italic, Artistic Script, and Myrtle Script, from *Book of Type Specimens*, Barnhart Bros. & Spindler's Type Founders, Chicago, 1910.

316–17. Specimen pages for Spinner Script, Great Primer, Double Pica, Double Columbian, and Ladies Hand Script No. 2 from Marder, Luse & Co., Type Founders, Chicago, date unknown.

318–19. Specimen pages for Stationer Script and Jewel Script from Farmer, Little & Co., Type Founders, Chicago, date unknown.

320. Specimen pages for Hoyt Script from the Cleveland Type Foundry, Cleveland, Ohio, 1910.

321. Specimen page for Keystone Pen Writer from the Keystone Type Foundry, Philadelphia, 1905.

322. Specimen page for Hazel Script from *Book of Type Specimens*, Barnhart Bros. & Spindler's Type Founders, Chicago, 1910.

323. Specimen page for Shepard Script Series from The Crescent Type Foundry, Chicago, 1895.

324–33 Specimen pages from selected foundries from *A Typographical Journey through the Inland Printer, 1883–1900*, compiled by Maurice Annenberg, Keystone Type Foundry, Philadelphia.

334–35. Ink-blotter advertisement for the Manhattan Life Insurance Company, New York, 1910.

336–39. Specimens of letterheads and scripts from Universal Engraving Company, New York, 1905.

340–41. Sampler letters; the original bitmapped typefaces from *The Jenny June Series of Manuals for Ladies, Letters and Monograms, for Marking on Silk, Linen and Other Fabrics*, 1889.

342–47 Script monograms, initials, and letterhead samples, found in a homemade scrapbook from Albany, New York, 1905 (collection of Louise Fili).

Annenberg, Maurice, *Type Foundries of America and their Catalogs*, New Castle, DE: Oak Knoll Press, 1994

Blackwell, Lewis, *Twentieth-Century Type*, New York: Rizzoli, 1992

Blackwell, Lewis, *Specimens of Printing Types Made at Bruce's New-York Type-Foundry*, New York: George Bruce's Son & Co., 1882

Cabarga, Leslie, *Progressive German Graphics, 1900–1937*, San Francisco: Chronicle Books, 1994

Cary, Melbert B., *Modern Alphabets*, Pelham, NY: Bridgman Publishers Inc., 1937 (3rd edn)

Day, Harold Holland, *Modern Brush Lettering*, Cincinnati, OH: Signs of the Times Publishing Co., 1931

Eason, Ron and Sarah Rookledge, *Rookledge's International Handbook of Type Designers: A Biographical Directory*, London: Sarema Press, 1991

Gress, Edmund G., *Fashions in American Typography 1780–1930*, New York: Harper & Bros., 1931

Harrison, John (ed.), *Posters & Publicity: Fine Printing and Design*, London: The Studio, 1927

Heller, Steven and Julie Lasky, *Borrowed Design: Use and Abuse of Historical Form*, London and New York: Van Nostrand Reinhold, 1993

Heller, Steven and Louise Fili, *Design Connoisseur: An Eclectic Collection of Imagery and Type*, New York: Allworth Press, 2000

Heller, Steven and Louise Fili, *Deco Type: Stylish Alphabets of the '20s and '30s*, San Francisco: Chronicle Books, 1997

Heller, Steven and Louise Fili, *Typology: Type Design from The Victorian Era to The Digital Age*, San Francisco: Chronicle Books, 1999

Heller, Steven and Anne Fink, *Faces on the Edge: Type in the Digital Age*, London and New York: Van Nostrand Reinhold, 1997

Hollis, Richard, *Graphic Design: A Concise History*, London: Thames & Hudson, 1994

Hollister, Paul M., *American Alphabets*, New York: Harper & Bros., 1930

Holme, C. G. (ed.), *Lettering of To-Day*, London: The Studio, 1937

Horsham, Michael, *20s & 30s Style*, London: Apple, 1989

Hutchings, R. S., *A Manual of Decorated Typefaces: A Definitive Guide to Series in Current Use*, London: Cory, Adams & Mackay, 1965

Johnston, Priscilla, *Edward Johnston*, London: Barrie and Jenkins, 1976 (2nd edn)

Meggs, Philip B., *A History of Graphic Design*, New York: John Wiley & Sons, 1998 (3rd edn)

Müller-Brockmann, Josef, *A History of Visual Communications*, New York: Visual Communication Books, Hastings House and Switzerland: Verlag Arthur Niggli, 1971

Poynor, Rick, *Typographica*, New York: Princeton Architectural Press, 2002

Sherraden, Jim, Elek Horvath and Paul Kingsbury, *Hatch Show Print: The History of a Great American Poster Shop*, San Francisco: Chronicle Books, 2001

Stevens, Thomas Wood, *Lettering*, New York: The Prang Company, 1916

Wallis, Lawrence W., *Modern Encyclopedia of Typefaces 1960–1990*, London: Lund Humphries, 1990

Welo, Samuel, *Practical Lettering: Modern and Foreign*, Chicago: F. J. Drake, 1930